HOW I TOOK A BARTENDING COURSE AND TRAVELED FOR SEVENTEEN YEARS

Steven Nicolle

 FriesenPress

Suite 300 - 990 Fort St
Victoria, BC, V8V 3K2
Canada

www.friesenpress.com

Copyright © 2017 by Steven Nicolle
First Edition — April 2014

I dedicate this book to my wife Soley whom I met on the ship and my two boys
Adam and Tomas. All three continue to give my life meaning. To others who have
helped me along the way I thank them as well. I am happy to share my story.

ISBN
978-1-4602-3898-1 (Hardcover)
978-1-4602-3899-8 (Paperback)
978-1-4602-3900-1 (eBook)

1. BIOGRAPHY & AUTOBIOGRAPHY, PERSONAL MEMOIRS

Distributed to the trade by The Ingram Book Company

Table of Contents

I dedicate this book to my wife Soley and my two boys Adam and Tomas, who give my life meaning each day.

Foreword

In 1979 I took a bartending course. Amazingly enough, there are still some of us around who do this for a living. Back then, being a bartender was a big deal in Montreal.

Bartending was a full-time job that many looked upon as a favourable occupation. You received full-time hours and, in many cases, it was a job that came with benefits.

A bartending job in a fine hotel required one to have taken some course in mixology before the hotel would even consider hiring you. Even with that course, in most cases, you would have to work up through the ranks to reach that coveted spot in front of a stool bar serving business people two-to-three hour martini lunches.

Nowadays though, I teach bartending and have noticed a lack of enthusiasm for the art of mixology. In 1979 the course I took was full. The past year we have not had enough people sign up to run the course. Granted, I do not live in a large urban center, but all we need is five people to sign up. That is not a large number by any means.

When you can Google a recipe for a Manhattan cocktail or take an online provincial accreditation that allows someone to serve alcohol to anyone of legal age without first knowing what is in the drink, why would anyone want to take a bartending course?

But now with people taking university courses and not being able to find work in their field of expertise and others whose employment has been terminated due to company relocation to a developing country, perhaps reconsidering that fun bartending course you always wanted to take might not be such a bad idea after all.

Then there is the social aspect.

Before there was Internet, and to a large extent cable television or cell phones, people interacted at their neighbourhood bar. Not just on a busy Saturday night, but every night. There was no texting or Facebook or Twitter. Just like back in the 1700s when people used to go to a pub or coffee house to meet others, it was still like that in 1979 when I started. People would go to a bar.

Except for the super rich, I think most people's spare income goes toward trying to keep up with their monthly payment on their cell phone and cable bills. I mean, why go out when you can sit at home and watch television and chat with friends that live next door on your cellphone?

Who actually would want to meet someone face-to-face and engage in a lively discussion, especially when the other may not share your point of view at all? I mean, walking out of a bar is a lot harder than disconnecting on Skype using a bathroom break as an excuse.

I have to admit the appeal of working unsociable hours is not a show-stopper for most people, but what position has social hours anymore? If you are not working, you are being hounded by text messages, emails, and voicemails when you are trying to relax.

At least when you bartend you head home when your shift is over with your gratuities and no one bothers you till you come back to work. There is a balance between life and work.

The bonus is if you stay long enough in this business and further educate yourself along the way you can become very good and make some excellent money. On top of that, your social life will become a whole lot better since you will not be home on Saturdays doing the same-old, same-old.

So unless you are in a prosperous field where you can do things that few others can do and there is a demand for your skill, you may be in the same boat I was back in 1979.

Let's face it: there is a difference between a university education and a high school education. I wish I had experienced a university education back when I could have, but I didn't.

But if right now you are looking for work, laid off, downsized, drowning in debt, lacking a social life, wanting to meet members of the opposite sex, yearning to travel, wanting more flexibility in the kinds of neighborhoods you can live in, then maybe just maybe you will consider that bartending course being offered after reading this book.

For me, life began with the bartending course. It led to me gaining experience as a Food Waiter as well as Sommelier. Management positions such as Assistant Food and Beverage Manager and Maitre'd. Not only did it lead me to various beautiful locations to live but it allowed me to meet some wonderful people. I am not sure anyone could ask for more. I grew in self confidence both professionally and personally. So sit back and let me tell you what happened.

Just a note: the names have been changed in my story to protect those who may not want their names to be mentioned.

Why Did I Take a Bartending Course Anyway?

The question I ask myself is, "why did I decide to take a bartending course, anyway?" Now that I teach bartending, I think I can come up with that answer.

Through my teenage years I was a bit of a loner. I had a few friends and just played sports. What I wanted to be since a very young age was a football player. In High School, I was quite the pass receiver, and was even invited to a junior camp run by the professional team in Montreal. It was the end, though, as I was too slow and skinny to compete with the bigger athletes.

Not knowing what I wanted to do after that, I jumped from job to job with only a small amount of money to show for my work each year. I would always wait till the end of February to get all my income statements so I could file my income tax and hopefully get a refund.

Basically, until the bartending course, the only jobs I did have were janitor jobs, shipper-receiver jobs, fork-lift, and truck driving jobs. Oh yes, and cleaning jobs. Loved cleaning toilets out and office cleaning–no, not really!

My first full time job was at Humpty Dumpty where my diet consisted of BBQ corn chips and potato chips. It was a couple of years after that before I could taste another one.

Other stellar jobs included working at a steering wheel automotive plant when, for eight hours, I would put defective steering wheels into an oven so the plastic would melt and then I would toss the frame into one bin and the plastic into another. I also worked on a paste line at a wallpaper plant.

I even tried my hand at selling pens that had the time and date flash on them. They went for a cool $19.95 back in 1978. I sold accident insurance, too.

In the new subdivisions where I lived, I sold two-inch storm doors for $249. The only problem was, there was a guy who bought them wholesale who sold the same door for $179.

I took courses in car repair that showed us how to actually work on a car. Remember the carburetor? Anyway, I discovered I didn't like getting my hands dirty. I took a course in Accounting, but that was too tedious. I tried my hand taking a course in Electronics, but dropped out halfway through.

Someone mentioned taking a Dale Carnegie course, so I spent $500. After the third class, I was so far ahead of the others in public speaking they wanted me to go for being an instructor. Rather than see that as an opportunity, I figured I didn't need it, so dropped out after the third class.

If you are like me, you are probably terrible at building things, so that rules out any trades that you would be good at doing. I tried to get into the police force, but flunked the psychology test. I even tried to get into the Armed Forces as a pilot, but flunked that test as well. Then, because I just wanted to be a pilot, I turned down a chance to go through training to become an Officer in the Navy.

I was also very stubborn.

Taking a bartending course was probably going to be a lot of fun and perhaps something would come of it, I hoped.

I also liked to drink. I would go out drinking at the bar and wake up in the morning to throw up before heading off to work. I always remember my mom asking from the bedroom if I was sick and my response was always, "I think I had some bad pizza last night."

At the time, I was eighteen and making Maalox in a pharmaceutical plant. We would get so far ahead of our work that in the afternoon I use to lay my hungover head behind the warm oven while the tablets were baking. Then I would finish the day and go out again that night. Yes, come to think of it, that happened on more than one occasion.

My greatest experience up to the bartending course was when I dropped out of John Abbott College in Montreal and went to Europe with my friend for 45 days. It was a blast traveling through all the countries. That made sense, as History and Geography were my two best subjects in school.

The only problem was, when I came back, I was in a different location from when I left. My folks had moved from Quebec to Ontario while I was in Europe. This move was typical during the mid-1970s when it looked like Quebec was on the verge of separating from the rest of Canada. I knew no one when I returned from Europe to Ontario. I returned to school and tried to get through Grade 13 in Ontario. I spent a month at school then dropped out.

Just over two years passed between the day I dropped out of school and the day I took the bartending course. During that time, I had over 25 jobs. The shortest job I had was a couple of hours and the longest one I had was 13 months. In that time, my folks moved back to Montreal and I stayed back in Ontario. After some time, I moved back to live with them in Montreal until they split up. At that time I moved out.

So in a nutshell, who takes a bartending course? If you are like me, you will drop out of school, travel to Europe, drink a lot, experience the split of your parents' relationship, move all over the place, have over 25 jobs, many of them dead-end, and fail to gain entry into the police or armed forces. All this in as little time as possible—like a couple of years.

How I Took a Bartending Course and Traveled for Seventeen Years

But one thing I was always doing was looking for something that might interest me. I didn't know quite what that something could be, but I figured if I didn't look, nothing would change. As I mentioned earlier, I had some sales experience during which time I learned of positive motivational books and tapes. I devoured those and I dare say it helped me quite a lot to understand myself and give me the strength to see further than my present circumstance. The books made me believe I was capable of doing anything, and I began to dream of a more exciting life.

So when I was glancing through the Montreal Star one day, I saw an ad about a bartending course at, of all places, McGill University. Hey, McGill is offering a bartending course. How cool was that!

I was a cool-looking 20-year old dude off to University in November of 1979. Well, okay, it was a bartending course, but at least I can say I went to University.

I really didn't know what to expect. I really think the only reason I took courses to begin with was in the hopes of meeting a girl. The first thing I always did was check out what females were in the class. At least if the course was boring I could try to get to know some new women.

Meeting women was always a bit of a challenge for me. I was quite shy in High School, even turning down a chance to take a girl to the graduation. Up to the time of the course I think I dated only two or three girls. Pretty pathetic really!

I think one of the thoughts I had was I couldn't quite figure the female gender out and anything I couldn't figure out I usually avoided. Also, I chose not to get into a relationship because I thought it would take too much up of my free time. My freedom was everything to me and halving my time with someone else seemed too much of an ordeal. The advantage I had with Bartending though was working with beautiful women. I knew I would eventually meet the right one. It took a few before I landed the right one but unlike other occupations it was okay to mess up. Sooner or later someone else would arrive on the scene. I didn't have to go out and look for someone.

At that moment I was working at a pharmaceutical plant in Montreal as a shipper-receiver and drove their truck to deliver and pick up raw materials. The most memorable thing or two I remember about that job was that I helped move the entire warehouse to a new location and empty these huge containers of sodium cyclamate that would arrive by ship from Taiwan. Twenty-five kilogram sacks stacked upon palette after palette. I think I must still hold the record for unloading the container the quickest. The boss used to marvel at my work ethic when it took me only 90 minutes to empty it.

It certainly wasn't something I wanted to pursue as a career, though, with the only hope being a possible promotion to an office job. That seemed a bit too boring for my liking. I thought that maybe the bartending course would change all that.

The Bartending Course

I was full of hope and aspiration as I briskly walked up McTavish Street, which ran adjacent to McGill University, that fall night. As fallen leaves crunched under the weight of my size 13 running shoes, my eyes looked for the building where the bartending course was going to be held for the next five Thursday evenings.

When I signed up for the course I never really thought of it as something to earn income. Although I went to a lot of bars and discotheques before this, my main interest in taking the bartending course was just to have some fun. It was a class you couldn't fail. There were no marks given or promises made after you finished the course. The investment I made in taking the course was a mere $48.00. All the glass and stainless steel shakers were included and it was real alcohol we were drinking. How much fun could that be!

A young guy was teaching the course. There were about 15 students in the class and what the teacher would have us do was sit in a U-shape and watch him talk and make a drink. He would give us notes on the drinks he was making and each of us would have a straw.

He would pass the drink to us and each of us would then have a sip. Over the course of an evening we hardly drank enough to feel the effects of the alcohol, but it was enough to give us an appreciation of how each cocktail should taste.

We tasted a Bloody Caesar that at that time had just come out on the market. That is like a Bloody Mary, but it used Clamato juice instead of simple tomato juice and it had celery salt around the rim of the glass. A Canadian invention, it has remained here for the most part. You can find it south of the border in places that cater to Canadian tourists.

There were the classic gin martini and manhattan cocktails. The funny thing was that back in 1979 you did not have the fancy flavoured martinis like the sour green apple martini or cosmopolitan like you have now. This was even before vodka became popular as a substitute for gin in a martini. It was gin, and that was it.

How I Took a Bartending Course and Traveled for Seventeen Years

Back in 1979, the young kids drank beer and shots. The men had their martini, manhattan, and Rob Roy cocktails, while the ladies would order their grasshoppers, Golden Cadillac, and pink lady. The last three cocktails are cream-based drinks that were big back then, but not so much now. They have been replaced by the popular frozen cocktails and aforementioned flavoured martinis.

There were no gadgets back then to crush the ice for you to make frozen cocktails. If you were lucky enough to have an ice machine that made crushed ice, you would only use it for the seldom-requested crème de menthe frappes. That was a shot of the liqueur over crushed ice. Frozen margaritas and pina coladas were unheard of. There were no pina colada or margarita premix for making them back then. Today everything is much more simplified.

So any drink you made, such as a pina colada, you had to make from scratch. First the rum, then the cream of coconut out of the Coco Lopez can, pineapple juice and a little cream and shake it. Pour that over ice in a tall glass and garnish with your slice of pineapple and cherry, and away you go.

Gin gimlets and daiquiris were big back then, but your daiquiri just consisted of a shot of rum and two-three ounces of lime bar mix. Remember, you couldn't have it frozen because there were no machines to crush that ice for you. So you would do the shake method with your stainless steel and glass shaker.

Nowadays, daiquiris are ordered in all flavours because of all the premixes available. With frozen drink ice machines all you do is add the alcohol, then the pre mix called for, and press a button. The button is for one or two drinks and the ice falls out and the machine does all the work for you. You simply pour afterwards. It is much easier than how I learned it.

Shooters really didn't get going till the early 1980s where they started in Alberta. So this course taught me little about layering different liquors on top of one another and downing them in a single gulp. I think it was about this time that Bailey's came onto the market, and when it arrived a whole bunch of different cream-based liqueurs followed. In the next few years, companies started introducing all sorts of stuff. I remember early on when I was bartending there was amaretto and cream and other concoctions that came and went. It was all the rage.

The only drink we learned how to layer was the pousse café. You would take a pony glass and layer different coloured liqueurs. The thicker liqueurs with the lower alcohol content went at the bottom and the lighter ones went on top. Usually it had five different colors in all. Then you would light the top of it upon presentation.

The fanciest drink we would make was a Singapore Sling, and you had to know how to make a zombie. The zombie was the drink that had two ounces of rum in it and fruit juices with some apricot brandy floating on too. That was the drink that people ordered if they wanted to get a quick buzz on. Today no one orders it anymore. I couldn't have imagined either when I made that Singapore Sling I would be sipping the same drink in Singapore years later.

Unlike anything I had ever done before, I had great fun learning how to mix drinks. Up to that point, I had hardly ever done anything creative in my life. But making a drink I could take raw materials and make a cocktail by shaking or stirring and pouring it into a glass then make it nice and pretty for presentation. It was simple to do and I became good at it.

So during the course, I bought bottles of liquor and borrowed some bar mix from the teacher and made drinks at home. I had already bought my stainless steel shaker and my glass shaker with the strainer. My mother was the guinea pig. I would make her some drinks and she would naturally say they were very good.

To get experience while I was taking the course, I got a job on Saturdays at the Jupiter discotheque at the Airport Hilton Hotel in Dorval, just outside of Montreal. I was the bar boy running stuff for the bartenders, making sure the fridges were full and keeping the bar area clean. At about 3:30 in the morning I would come home feeling exhilarated.

It was nice to be part of the action and excitement of a nightclub and not have to worry about asking anyone to dance. Before, I use to go to discotheques and get constantly turned down when asking girls to dance. It was a big show back in the disco days. People would go out all dressed up and just sit there and gawk at one another. It wasn't really my scene, but I could definitely work in a place like that and enjoy the music.

I recall that there would always be a certain moment during the night when a song use to play and everyone would hit the dance floor. That song I recall was "Funky Town." It came out early in 1980 and the bass was pretty heavy.

The bartenders who were in their 40s would be non-stop making drinks. You could see the perspiration on their forehead popping out as the bar would get about two-three deep with people yelling over the music for another drink. That disco used to rock. The ladies were all dressed up and the men all walked around with the top button on their shirt open to make them feel macho.

Yes, you could say I was pretty hooked on the whole scene back then. It was far more exciting than filling out orders in a warehouse or working on an assembly line, and from what I heard, the money was pretty good when you became a bartender. In fact, working those Saturday nights, I made more as a bar-boy on a per-hour basis than I did working at my full-time job.

So, as the bartending course went on, I began to think of this as a career choice. I talked to people in the class to see what they were going to do after the course finished. Some had jobs lined up and others were there just like I was at the beginning, just checking the course out.

That is when I met this student who gave me my first break in the bartending industry. From then on, my life became far from boring, you could say.

An Early Failure

It was January of 1980 and it was coming near the end of the bartending course. It was time to see if I could capitalize on what I had learned and continue my enthusiasm for making cocktails.

I had just recently rented a studio apartment where I got the first month free if I did the cleaning before I moved in. The landlord was really lazy, but I gladly took the free month and my mom and I cleaned the place out. It was a real mess. I owned a 1971 big Oldsmobile Delta 88 with a 455 under the hood. It was massive. So I had a car, my apartment, and was ready to rumble, so to speak.

Moving out was not on my list of things to do at the time, because when I moved back to Montreal from Brampton, Ontario to stay with my mom and stepfather, it was with the hope that I might save a bit of money. I liked Montreal too, as that is where I grew up and where my friends were, so it made a lot of sense.

However, shortly after moving back, my stepfather then declared he was moving out. So it was Mom and I, all of a sudden. I felt like I was in the middle of this drama, so I moved out a couple of weeks later. They ended up moving back and forth together for a couple of years and then it was all too much and they divorced. The bartending course was perfect timing, you could say, as it was sort of an escape from a lot of things that were going on.

Now, bartending is not one of those occupations where you just go to school and get the knowledge and check yourself into a fine job. You do not graduate out of it with any mark as such. It is just your willingness to go on to the next step that matters. There are few who take a bartending course and pursue it for any length of time. Just the insecurity of having no clear path ahead once you finish the course stops a lot of people from moving forward. However adventure and risk to me were pretty exciting. It served me well in finding work in the Hospitality Industry no matter the obstacles put before me. Besides I loved Bartending. I was devouring recipe books wherever I could get my hands on them. It was a beginning for me and I was determined to make it happen.

I got a look at what it was like as a bar boy at the discotheque, but those 40 year old bartenders were not going anywhere soon. So I needed to find another way to break in the business.

Networking while taking the bartending course, I met the owner of a very successful pub at the time called the Willows Inn in Hudson, Quebec. He was there only to improve his drink knowledge. We started talking about the business and he noticed how interested I was in becoming a bartender. On the last day, he gave me his business card and told me to give him a call in the next few weeks. The spring season was starting up and they would be hiring soon.

I didn't wait long. I called and he suggested I come in for a slow shift to tend bar. It was going to be on a Monday. "Fine," I said, "I can do that!"

Well, I can remember getting behind the bar and being ready to have those 12 seats filled. I got there about five PM. It was happy hour, and drinks were two for the price of one. It wasn't that busy, but I recall that there was one guy who threw up at the bar and another got into a loud argument with another patron. The scene was kind of chaotic at times, and Frank guided me nicely through the minefields. Mostly, I was pouring draft beer and some shots, but for a first time, I was pretty excited.

Afterwards, Frank took me aside and started apologizing for what had transpired. Usually there weren't people sick at the bar and fighting words weren't usually exchanged between guests, he told me. I believed him because the Willows Inn already had a pretty good reputation for visitors coming in from out of town. In fact, I had been there before as a paying customer, so I knew that already.

He thought I did pretty well at the bar and asked me if I would consider coming on full-time. "Of course," was my reply, and the next day I gave my two weeks notice at the pharmaceutical company where I was a shipper-receiver and truck driver.

Well, the good thing about Frank was he got me my first start and that I will always be grateful for, but the bad thing was when I started a couple of weeks later, he was nowhere to be found.

My first shift was as a waiter, which I hardly knew anything about. I arrived and was given a section. Before I could get acquainted with the menu and table numbers, we were slammed. It was spring and the sun was out and everyone in town was coming for lunch.

I made mistake after mistake. It was a disaster and at the end I was pretty subdued. What the heck just happened! First of all, no one told me I was going to be a food waiter. I had no training on the floor. I got the table numbers mixed up. I rang in the wrong orders. The rest of the staff was as busy was I was, so they really did not have any time to help. Basically, I was screwed!

After the shift I found out Frank had sold the place and I was now working for the new guys. They knew nothing of me and probably just put me on the schedule on Frank's request.

I worked a couple of weeks after that first day, and then I was told I was being let go. That was it. My first job was an abject failure. Sure I got some experience, but I was out of work. What was I going to do? I had left my job at the warehouse and my job as bar boy at the Hilton.

Now you would think it would have been easy to find another job in the industry, but in Quebec that was not the case, especially if you did not know how to converse in French.

When the Separatist party gained power back in 1977, they put in a law called Bill 101. This draconian law stated that everything had to be in French: from signs to what language you were greeted in when you went shopping. I remember a couple of years earlier my mother was let go from her retail job because a secret shopper had complained that her French was not good enough.

Anyway, the point is that if a person did not know how to speak French they were pretty much out of luck in finding a job in Quebec. I had the one in Hudson, which was far enough away that you could get away with using English only. But now that that was over, I had to look for something closer to the city.

With rent to pay and no job, I knocked on doors everywhere. My next job was as a busboy in a fine dining restaurant on Crescent Street in Montreal, Le Troika. Not exactly the bartending job I was looking for, but a job nonetheless. It was a Russian restaurant. I remember the maître d' was French, the chef Arabic, the owner Jewish. I mean, if war was to break out, I thought this would be a heck of a place to work!

Although they were helpful, I felt way out of my league there. In hindsight, many years later realize I was given a great opportunity to work on the busiest nightclub and eating-out area in all of Montreal. All I needed to do was take a French course and really learn everything about fine dining right there. This place used to fly in their fresh fish catch of the day for heaven's sake! White linen, fine China, table-side service, and the list goes on. The clientele were high paying guests who would come for their caviar and champagne.

But I guess you could say that my desire to be a bartender won out. When you are young, you are stubborn. I had no experience to draw on except for a handful of shifts at the Willow Inn.

Besides that, there was the break-up and constant drama going on between my mother and stepfather. Most of my friends had packed up and moved out of the province due to the threat of Quebec leaving Canada. Businesses too had packed up and moved their headquarters out of Montreal to Toronto and other big Canadian cities. Some had moved out altogether. Unemployment was surging. Job prospects were not good, no matter what field you were in.

So with all that, I decided to head back to Ontario. I gave my step-brother a call to see if I could crash out at his place until I got a job and a place to stay. He accepted my request and I quickly found myself back in Brampton where I would find much greater success finding work.

Back To Ontario

It was May of 1980 when I left Montreal for Brampton, Ontario to search for a bartending job and stay with my step-brother and his wife. Leaving my apartment behind, the plan was to get a job and then come back and pick up my things and give a month's notice. I wanted to keep the apartment for the time being back in Montreal as a place to store stuff until I got a place of my own.

The only concern I had about this move was leaving my car back in Montreal to be fixed. It needed a new radiator at the time and since I didn't have the money to fix it, I left it in the good hands of my step-father, who promised that he would get it repaired. I would simply return to pay him back then drive it back to Brampton.

My job hunt consisted of getting up early enough to grab a bus to get to where I was going to look for work. Back in 1980, the closest action was not in Brampton, but Airport Road, which was about an hour away by bus. In fact, the bus would drop me off at the Airport Terminal and then I would hike it back to the row of hotels that were lined up one after the other.

Instead of going to the Human Resource department to fill out an application, I would go to the bar or restaurant and just ask for the maître d' or anyone who was in charge during my visit. I needed to find work quickly, so that is what I did– bypass the Human Resource Department. I hoped I would make a good impression and be recommended by someone who already worked there.

One of my first stops was the Holiday Inn. They did not have a nightclub, but they did have the Roof Garden Restaurant, and I had heard they might be looking for a service bartender. I walked in and asked for the manager. The maître d' approached and listened to my story. I told him I had taken a bartending course in Montreal, but had limited experience. Relocating back to Brampton, I was looking to get my foot in the door with some hotel.

I remember his name was Alex. He was from Greece. We chatted and he took a liking to me and disclosed that, yes, there was an opening coming up in the service bar of the restaurant. It was serving drinks to 2-4 waiters and the hourly wage was $6.95 an hour. The waiters would tip me out, but not much. We agreed the experience would be very helpful.

He phoned the Human Resource Department and told them I would be coming down to do all the paperwork and I would be starting the following

Monday. My shifts were lunches from 10-3. That was Monday to Friday, Saturday off and then I would do a double on Sunday.

The one thing I had to do was to come in a couple of evening shifts and watch the nighttime guy and learn how he made the cocktails.

Later that week, I came to work with a notepad in hand ready to watch an old pro make some cocktails. He was late-40s, early-50s and you could tell just by looking at him that he had been preparing cocktails for quite a number of years. The waiters too were around the same age and they all had emigrated from Europe. There I was, 21 years old and as green as grass compared to these guys.

Nowadays, when I see a young person with relatively little experience enter the bar or dining room it takes me back to my early years. I was just hoping someone like Alex would give me a chance. There is no real safety net for the novice. Only his or her willingness to learn and enthusiasm get them by those first few shifts. Without those two attributes the new person usually doesn't last very long.

It was easy enough I thought. The drinks were pretty easy to make and he made it clear that working lunches would not be as busy as working dinners, so I should not find myself backed up in drink orders. If I had a question, the waiters would help me out. Everyone was very helpful. Another thing he mentioned was not to give anyone any drinks without ringing them up first. "Absolutely," I replied back.

The following Monday I arrived earlier than I needed to so I could get the bar requisition, cut the fruits, and make the juices. Alex was there and asked if I was ready. He opened the doors and it was all very exciting for me.

I was very grateful to be working and getting a shot at bartending. The waiters, though, were difficult. You see, back in 1980 it seemed like everyone drank on the job and management would just turn the other cheek. Nowadays, if you are caught drinking, you are more likely to be fired right on the spot.

Now there I was trying to follow the rules and only make drinks that had been rung up. The waiters, though, would try to get me to make them a drink. They would flash a two-dollar bill in front of me. I begged them to leave me alone and just let me do my job.

Then they would tell me the night guy did it all the time and how else do you think he can make a living if he didn't take some money on the side? I wondered, sure, but what if I got caught? Then it dawned on me, Alex never came back to check on anything. I thought I could use the extra cash.

So I capitulated and poured a shot for one of the waiters and took the money. But instead of hiding it he puts it right out there so if anyone walked in they would immediately notice. I was sweating bullets as he reassured me not to worry!

Each shift I would do the same. It wasn't the right thing to do. I even took a drink when one asked me what I would like to have. He gave me a couple of bucks just so I would pour myself one.

It was insane, but what was even more insane was I was taking this stupid bus each day and I needed my car. I called my stepfather up and asked if the car was fit to drive. My mom answered and apparently he had looked at it and it was ready for the six-hour drive.

I was going to take the overnight bus on Friday night and arrive Saturday morning. That is what I did so I could drive it back Saturday and have it for work Sunday.

Getting off the smoke-filled bus (in those days you could smoke on the bus), I finally caught up with my stepfather to grab the keys off him. He said I didn't need a new radiator and instead he just ran some fluid through the cooling system that was supposed to plug up any leaks. I knew it needed a new radiator, so I was pretty upset he didn't get it replaced. "It will be fine," he answered back. "Sure!" I thought.

Meanwhile, the landlord had put some of my stuff in a locker, as he wasn't sure if the rent was going to be paid. I assured him it would be and it was. On my next trip back I got my stuff, thus completing the move to Ontario.

Driving the car back was a nightmare. Not even 35 minutes out, the temperature light was on and I was at a gas station. I phoned my stepfather up. "Thanks a lot!" I screamed.

Thirteen hours and many stops later, I got home. An overnight bus ride the night before and then the arduous drive back. I worked the double shift on Sunday. I took the car to the auto shop on Monday. The mechanic couldn't believe I had driven the car from Montreal in the condition it was.

Looking back, of course the whole move thing could have been handled a bit differently. I was the sort of person, though, that if I wanted something, I did my best to get it. I wanted to be a bartender, and the opportunity was not going to happen in Montreal after the Willow Inn let me go. So, on impulse I packed up and went to where I could get something. I didn't have hardly any money, a car at the beginning to look for work, nor hardly any experience. I did find the Holiday Inn, though, and I was getting good at making cocktails.

I don't think I talked to my stepfather after that. I may have seen him once or twice in a shopping mall when I went back to Montreal on a visit. So I lived with him from the time I was eight till I was 18 years of age with four other stepsisters. I haven't seen or talked to any of them since the early 80s. Then, on top of that, I lost contact with a lot of friends who moved away the previous couple of years; it was a time for letting go of the past, although, as you will see, it was hard to say goodbye to Montreal the city.

I moved into a furnished room in a big house in Brampton where the rent was $35 a week. Low enough that I could start saving some money.

Well, you may think that now I was going to be at the Holiday Inn for a number of months or years. But the fact was, I was there only three weeks. Yes, I know that sounds ridiculous. I even gave two weeks notice on top of it. So literally, I lasted one week! What happened was I got a phone call. It was June of 1980.

A Call From a Friend

One of the things I will always be thankful for is that, throughout my time working, I have received a lot of help. There I was working as a service bartender at the Holiday Inn. Alex the maître d' liked me enough to give me a chance, as did Frank (from my bartending class) when he hired me at the Willow Inn earlier that spring.

But what I didn't expect was help from yet another person. To explain, I will go back a couple of years. When I first moved to Brampton from Montreal with the family, one of my jobs was working at this pharmaceutical plant as a material handler. My responsibility was working on the packaging line. I use to chat with all the women while performing the mundane repetitive task of filling cartons, taping them up, and loading them onto a skid.

Well, as it turned out, there were soon going to be lay-offs, and I was going to be one of them. This woman, Carla, recommended that I check out where her son Gordon worked. I followed her advice and got a job at a factory where wallpaper was made.

I worked there for a few months, then moved back to Montreal. When I returned to Brampton and was working at the Holiday Inn, I called back a few people to tell them I was back in town.

One of those people was Carla. Over the phone, she began to tell me that her husband, Mr. D, was in the hospitality industry and had been for many years. Well, not a week later, I got a call from him telling me he needed a head bartender at this private golf club and would I mind coming aboard.

At this point, I had hardly been at the Holiday Inn at all, and to tell them I was going to leave seemed a bit mean and unfair to Alex. One thing Mr. D was good at, though, was selling the idea.

Unlike being in the background as I was at the Holiday Inn, I would be in the front serving drinks to the members. I would have some additional responsibilities, such as maintenance of the bar, ordering supplies, and requisitioning. The hours were flexible and in the end there would be more hours and money. Also, it would be hard to pass up a couple of square meals a day that would save me eating out at restaurants all the time.

I took the job right there over the phone, and with much trepidation, the next day gave my two-weeks notice to Alex. He wasn't too happy, but understood why I needed to go. He was even nice enough to give me a letter of recommendation, although who would ever read it? I worked there for a total of just over 3 weeks.

The Credit Valley Golf Club was a real fun place to work. It was fun because when I was serving members they treated me pretty good. They made me feel welcome and I got to know them after a very short time.

Let's face it, golf isn't exactly something I did and got all worked up over. The nineteenth hole was located right where I stood—at the bar, that is. It wasn't hard work, but I was getting the experience that I lacked—pouring drinks right in front of the person. If I made a mistake, it was not a big deal.

The great thing about working in a private club is all the money that a member pays goes back into the club. A club would never fret over a mistake, unlike a public bar. The membership fee a member has to pay to join and then the monthly dues upon acceptance guarantees a huge cash flow. Clubs are set up as non-profit. They are there for the member. Whatever the member wants, they get. So for me, or any other bartender starting out, it was a great training ground. I highly recommend it.

Mr. D made sure I was well taken care of. Food and drink were abundant. I got paid a decent wage and with the overtime I put in, I was managing, for the first time, to put some money away. Life was good.

There was only one problem. Mr. D did not get along with the manager. I tried to ignore what was going on and hoped that it would pass.

The drinking by the staff was evident as well. I remember one month the inventory showed that we went through 5 kegs of beer, but the sales showed we only sold a half keg's worth. I always knew if the manager was coming around, because someone would warn others to get their empty beer mugs to the bar so I could dispense with them in the glass washer. Also, the cigarettes were for the members only, but by the end of the month I had so many IOU notes I had to make sure everyone returned what they had took so the inventory would come out alright.

Mr. D was a heck of a nice guy, and probably as food and beverage manager he should have been leading the charge against drinking draft beer and borrowing cigarettes, but he liked to smoke and drink himself. When the manager was off, everyone would sit in the chef's office during the slow mid-afternoon or after the dinner rush and eat and drink. This wasn't work at all, I thought. We all would chat about anything and everything.

By eleven o'clock at night the bar would give last call. They were not late nights. I'd count the liquor empties, check the beer fridge, and make the requisition out. All the while sipping on a nice cocktail.

It was the summer of 1980 in Canada. Terry Fox was beginning his run, which tragically ended in Thunder Bay. Everything was cheap. Food, gas, and lodging were affordable. I was living in that 35 dollar a week room and saving a bunch of cash. I didn't have any real plans for the future. I enjoyed tending bar, and despite the unsociable hours, I didn't miss anything by working days and nights. I was single with no girlfriend. I liked my life uncomplicated. I was having some fun for the first time in a while.

Then one day in October I came into work and got the news Mr. D had left. He didn't like the manager and decided to move on. A couple of days later, I gave him a call and he was on the lookout for another job. He said that once he got one he would be bringing me along with him. I thanked him a lot for what he had done for me already and emphasized that he need not do anything else for me.

But a month later I received another phone call....

The Top Arrives Suddenly Then Disappears

It was only the previous fall that I had taken the Bartending Course and there I was, already a head bartender at an elite golf club. I was feeling pretty good about the situation I found myself in. Then Mr. D, who got me the job, suddenly departed with the promise he would call me once he found a place. It was nice of him, but to be honest, it didn't matter, as I was quite happy at the golf club.

Still, as promised, about a month after he left I got a call from Mr. D. He was now working at the Bristol Place Hotel on the airport strip in their fine dining restaurant as a captain. Then he said that the nightclub on the top floor was looking for a bartender and that he put in a good word for me to Gord, the Bar Manager. All I had to do was give Gord a call to set up an interview, but I had to act fast because the spot was open right now and they needed one in a hurry.

I was getting some good experience making cocktails behind the bar at this point in time. But I had only been bartending for about six months in total. The Bristol Place was looking for someone who had a minimum of five years experience. Mr. D tried to ease my anxiety by saying I could do it and that this bar was the top of the line. "Just give Gord a call."

So I did, and we set up a time to meet. The interview went okay, but I guess I didn't inspire that much confidence as Gord put off any decision to hire me right on the spot. I gave Mr. D a call and told him of what transpired and thanked him for the opportunity. Like I said, it wasn't a life or death situation for me as I was happy where I was.

The next thing I knew, Gord called me up and told me I had the job. I was kind of surprised, until I found out Mr. D went to Gord and gave him shit for not hiring me right there. I guess Gord had no choice but to give me a call. You could say Mr. D had some pull.

By this time, it was December and the Christmas parties were beginning and here I was giving my two-weeks notice. I worked at the club till Christmas and my first day to start at the Bristol Place was New Year's Eve of all nights.

How I Took a Bartending Course and Traveled for Seventeen Years

The layout of the bar was superb. The top of the bar was mirror and had about 10 stools. There were three round tables behind the stools where another twelve people could sit. On Friday and Saturday nights the bar would be two-three deep with people all at the same time wanting a drink. There was a service bartender that would work from nine till closing on Friday and Saturday nights making the drinks for four cocktail waitresses.

It was a pretty swanky bar with business people during the week and hot looking ladies. On Friday and Saturday nights the crowd changed from the traveling corporate clientele to the disco crowd. On those nights I never stopped making drinks. My sales for a Saturday night would go over a $1000, which back then was quite a bit of work.

A three-ounce martini I remember was $5.95. A beer would go for less than $3. A shot was $3.50. I remember I used to have a bunch of tabs going at the same time and one guy every Friday would come in and tell me to buy the bar a round on his tab. So I would have to giddy up and make at least a dozen cocktails right there and then.

I was making some excellent money and gaining tons of confidence. I remember when I started I was a little worried. First of all, starting New Year's Eve was a bit of a scare, but it really wasn't that busy. The nightclub sold packages, and if anyone out there reading knows about New Year's Eve packages, they are usually well overpriced and subsequently undersold.

Doing inventory that night till four in the morning with Gord was quite the experience. We chatted together. I had a few drinks, but he drank a bottle of Scotch all by himself. Haig Pinch was the Scotch and if you can't recall the Scotch, you may remember the irregular shape of the bottle it comes in.

Now, if you can imagine, I had been bartending since June of 1980 and now it was the beginning of 1981 and I was working at a bar where you needed at least five years of experience. I was handling my own, but I was still pretty young. If it wasn't for Mr. D, there was no way I would have got this job.

You see, working in a bar where the people were at least twice as old as I was was not that easy. It was not at all comfortable because they had seen a bit of life and I was still young. You try to have anything in common with them. It was like selling houses or life insurance without owning a house or having life insurance. It can be hard to connect with the other person. That is how I felt.

Sure, it was a great bar and I was making some good coin, but I wasn't totally having fun. My hours one week would be from eleven to seven from Monday to Friday and the following week from seven to close Tuesday to Saturday. It just seemed I would be coming home from work late at night, then getting up and getting a bite to eat and heading back.

I came to realize that the hours were not all that sociable either. I never saw my friends, or should I say acquaintances, anymore. Family became distant. Instead of meeting people, I was becoming more of a loner.

There were some storm clouds on the horizon. Sure, it was at the time a prestige bartending job. I mean, it was just a little over a year earlier that I was watching the 40-year old bartenders at the Jupiter Discotheque where I was a bar boy and I was thinking of how cool a job that would be. There I was in the same position in so little time.

It was about this time I started to drink more. It just wasn't a beer or two now, but it was hard liquor. Last call would take place at one o'clock and the place would be empty a half hour later. I would stick around and do my cash out and choose between having a Black Russian, a rusty nail, a stinger, a rye and ginger, or whatever else I felt like. Then I'd hand my deposit in around 2:30.

On the way home I would grab a bite to eat, then hit the pillow close to four in the morning. It was not the healthiest lifestyle.

At work it was pretty funny because if I wanted something good to eat I would have to get one or two strong rum and cokes to the Chef. Well I couldn't leave the bar to give it to him and he just couldn't walk out and grab one so the busboy was the middleman. He used to take the dirty glasses from the bar and take them to the back to the glass-washer machine. Walking by, the busboy would ask me what I wanted for lunch and tell the chef. I'd pour a stiff rum and coke and leave it on the dirty glass tray. A glance and a wink later, he was taking the dirty glass tray back to the kitchen. I'd get my steak.

I recall on my twenty-first birthday I was scheduled to be off at 7 PM. I figured on going out afterwards. Then I found out the night guy was not coming in, so the manager asked if I would take a two-hour break and come back at nine to close. Feeling choked, I went to this Chinese Food Restaurant and had some egg rolls and belted back about six Black Russians. Then, on my way back to work, I hit a checkerboard sign. It was drizzly and the wipers on my car were smudging my view. I didn't realize I was in a left turn lane and hit the sign.

I pulled over with a cop car not far behind. I talked my way out of it by saying I had to get back to work while blaming the hit on the windshield wipers. He was nice enough and let me go. I was getting fed up with my situation. Sure, it was a good job, but I didn't have much else going.

Then I did a stupid thing. On a super busy Saturday night in March right at closing time, the night club manager told me to go ahead and start cleaning up and that he would count my cash for me. I said, "Sure, go ahead."

He counted the cash, separated the float and put aside what was left for the service bartender and I. On a night when we should have made a fair chunk of change we had 40 dollars each leftover. Now, whether or not he did it right, there was no way we could have made so little. I mean, the tip out from the waitresses would have been at least 30-40 dollars.

It was a huge error on my part. How could I let someone else do my cash out?

Bottom line was I couldn't work for this guy anymore. Gord had since been let go so I couldn't bring it up to him. Mr. D, upon hearing the news, was angry and disappointed. I couldn't sleep anymore over it.

I had to leave and cut bait. I went in on the Monday, gave a one-day notice, and said goodbye. I was upset at the way things had turned out. The other bartender had left a week earlier so the manager was in the shit you could say. From what I heard, he was let go a couple of months later.

That was the way it was in those days. People came and went overnight, it seemed. There were a lot of situations going on and when it came to alcohol and money, there was always some trouble not far behind.

In a year I had worked at five jobs and moved from Montreal back to Ontario. It was not unusual to go through a lot of jobs when you started out in the Hospitality Industry back in the early 80's because there were a lot of jobs available. It is one industry where you only gain experience by switching jobs often. I had the good fortune of having some help finding the jobs I had up to then.

As with all good things, though, they do come to an end and having that manager count my cash that night led to a personal spiral over the next couple of years.

I never worked again with Mr. D, but what a great friend. He, more than anyone, helped me big time with two jobs that really accelerated my bartending experience. He worked at the Bristol Place till he retired.

Now I had to find a job again. "It shouldn't be that difficult," I thought, "after my experience working at the Bristol Place Hotel."

Disco Fever at 5444

It was April of 1981 and I was without a job again. My changes in employment over the past year did not look good on my resume and there was no way I could use my last employer as a reference either, having given only one day's notice.

Despite that, I wasn't too worried because the jobs in the newspaper were abundant. There were loads of places looking for bartenders. It was the peak of the disco scene. I ended up finding a job at the Ramada Inn in their discotheque, 5444. The number was the address. How original is that?

What had happened was the previous bartenders had all been let go and they were looking for a whole new crew. I just happened to pop in at that time. The period between leaving the previous job and finding this one was a little over a week. Chris, who was the manager, hailed from New York City where he had a stint at the Playboy Club. He was lean, had an Afro hairdo, and a goatee to boot. The disco was on two floors with really nice sofas and a lightshow worth a hundred thousand dollars that overlooked the dance floor.

The bar was huge. Two bartenders would work the wood on the weekends and another would make the cocktails for the waitresses. I was the only guy who worked there, so I enjoyed the female company.

I liked working in the discotheque. Opening at 4 pm for the cocktail crowd, we offered some hot hors d'oeuvres along with some reasonably-priced cocktails to encourage the hotel guests to come. But the real fun took place when the disc jockey started blasting some tunes. It was party-time every night.

I remember Chris organized a swimsuit contest one night. After each shift we would hang around the bar and have a few drinks, then head to a 24-hour restaurant until the sun started to come up. Then it was time to head home and get some sleep.

I was the designated head bartender, so I was the one who had to show the new hires the ropes.

The system I had put into place was quite simple for anyone to follow. The only thing was, it was not honest. You see, I didn't entirely agree with the price list. I thought it was confusing. The point-of-sale system was the popular NCR machine.

The keys on the machine would include domestic beer, imported beer, bar brands, premium brands, cocktails, and so on. The price list was posted near the machine so we could see what the cost of the drink was and punch the appropriate key.

When I saw the price list, I noticed they had divided the cocktails into price tiers. You could order a cocktail, a premium cocktail, or a deluxe cocktail. For example, a Tom Collins was a basic cocktail, a Singapore Sling was a premium cocktail, and a deluxe cocktail would be a basic cocktail with a premium brand alcohol substituting the bar brand. It was pretty confusing. Either that, or I just couldn't be bothered to look at the price list. Maybe it was the latter reason. Now, come to think of it, it was!

The reason I was able to do this is I had complete and utter control of the bar. I was there all the time. My days off were the Sunday and Monday it was closed.

Another thing to remember is everyone drank like fishes. Chris would be at the door every half hour holding up his empty glass asking for a rye and coke. Jack, the Disc Jockey, would ask for his screwdriver, and I would float about 3 ounces of Vodka on top so he would get a quick buzz. The bartenders were all drinking.

But each month the inventory would come out all right. "How could this be?" I wondered.

Well, for one thing, I charged the deluxe price for most cocktails. The way I figured it, if it had two kinds of liquors in it, I priced it as deluxe. A single liquor cocktail was a premium. The lowest price I eliminated.

So basically the guests were overcharged and we would short pour at the service bar. All so we could party. The consequences of that I didn't find out till later. I really didn't know how liquor cost worked at the time. I just figured as long as your par stock was good and no bottles went missing, everything would turn out all right.

I remember one time there was this new girl who served a drink to someone and followed the price list before I could tell her. The guest called me over and asked why he was charged less for his drink than what he normally paid. I had to smooth talk my way out of it and tell the new hire how we charged for the drinks.

Honestly, I have to say looking back it was real dishonest of me to even think of doing what I did. I made my own price list disregarding the one posted. But, at the same time, I saved everyone's butt without even realizing it. Chris, the DJ, and the staff all drank like fishes. The drinking was over the top. Way too much.

It was a pretty fast life I was leading and then all of a sudden I wanted to shack up with this girl in Toronto who worked with me. I was ready to move to the big city with her. She was like a flower child right out of the 70s. I don't know why, but I always went for the live free women in those days. The total opposite of myself! I was way too serious back then.

So I left this job thinking that when she came back from her holiday in Vancouver she and I were going to shack up together in downtown Toronto. Like a moron, I found a place in downtown Toronto anticipating her eventual return from Vancouver. That was November of 1981. I figured it would be easy to find a place to work downtown.

Well, she never came back, except once. She came for a visit and we went to the Swiss Chalet. I realized then it might have been a blessing she stayed out west.

She ordered a double Dubonnet on the rocks. Usually a single Dubonnet is a three- ounce pour. When they brought a highball to her filled to the brim, I kind of thought maybe this wouldn't be the right girl with which to shack up.

Many years later, while I was living in Vancouver, I saw a girl that bore a striking resemblance to this one and was tempted to say hello and ask her if she came from Toronto, but I passed up the opportunity. It's pretty funny how things in our lives seem to go in circles.

Unfortunately for Chris and the staff, my departure soured things for them. A couple of months later, I returned for a visit and Chris told me the liquor costs were out of control and management was coming down hard on him.

As he held a rye and coke in his hand, I told him I didn't know what was wrong, but if there was something he could do it was to tell everyone to stop drinking, or at least cut down. I was one to talk. That night I must have had about 17 rye and ginger ales without paying a dime.

A couple of months later, I got the news the entire team and Chris got the boot. I knew it was inevitable, because one thing Chris couldn't do was toe the line with the staff. They give him an ultimatum: fire everyone or he would be fired too. A great guy. It was unfortunate to see it end that way for him.

As for myself, I soon discovered that my frequent changing of jobs was catching up with me. So was my drinking. A bad mixture was brewing.

Going From Job to Job and Place to Place

It was December of 1981 and I had just moved to Toronto to go and work in a bar. I had the plan of moving in with this girl when she got back from Vancouver, so I found an apartment downtown that went for $275 a month.

I remember my grandfather died around that time and I picked up a couple of chairs and a table that was left behind to fill the new apartment. The apartment was a big room with a kitchenette on the side, and a bathroom. The one thing that stands out in my mind about that dumpy place was it had a small window that looked out directly to the building beside me three feet away. What a view! Another memory of that apartment is how the radiator never gave me any heat.

The janitor told me that it might help to bleed the radiator a bit. I took that valve and turned it a bit, then a bit more, and then a bit more. Suddenly, the valve came right off and hot water came spewing out. I waited for about 20-30 seconds then realized that the hot water was not going to stop. I had to try to get the valve back on! Hard to do when hot water is bursting out all over against you. Finally, I got it back on, but not before a puddle was created in the living room. The janitor got a water vacuum and cleaned it up. The room, needless to say, had the stench of a jungle after a downpour with all the humidity filling the air. It felt like it lasted a long time.

In the year of 1982 there was a shift in the economy. Jobs were no longer easy to come by due to the recession that was taking place. My resume was pretty tattered as well. I ended up at jobs that didn't pay. I really had no job references, understandably, after the short time I spent at each place I worked. So I was left with just trying to make a good impression.

One thing I did become rather good at was doing interviews. By this time, I had become experienced at asking the right questions and providing the right answers. So I still ended up getting jobs. The only thing was, the jobs I got were not the best choices.

I got this bartending position at this new restaurant that made fancy drinks with dry ice. Smoke would roll off the top of the drink. It was all well and good, but opening day was such a disaster that I couldn't work there anymore. At another job I worked as an assistant to the manager. Sounded like a great opportunity, but I didn't really know what I was doing. I lasted a week there.

I had a job offer to bartend at this women's club downtown that was just opening up and for some stupid reason I turned it down. I should have, just for the women!

Opportunities were out there for me and obviously the people who were hiring believed in me, but maybe I didn't quite believe in myself enough. It sounds a bit too cliché, but if you don't know what it is you want, then how can anyone be of use to you? I just didn't know what I wanted. I suffered from a lack of focus.

My relatives were all doing their thing. I had moved to Toronto on the spur of the moment partly because of what people thought I should do and not what I wanted to do. I thought I could go to Toronto and work in some swanky bar again, but I discovered that there were people downtown who had their connections, like I once had back in Brampton. The jobs I wanted were the ones like at the Bristol Place where you needed five years experience. The only difference was someone else got me that job at the Bristol Place. On my own and with my history, there was not a chance.

I ended up at the Badminton Racquet Club right off Yonge Street in Toronto. It was an hourly wage with no gratuities. Not exactly what I was looking for. In the middle of the year, the jobs had dried up. The help wanted ads were miniscule and if you applied for work anywhere there were line-ups. Interest rates were skyrocketing and restaurants were closing left, right, and center.

The racquet club was quite a spot to work. All we did was drink. The members used to have what was called a club size cocktail. The cocktail was three ounces. Martinis, rusty nails, stingers all were served in a huge old fashion glass filled with shaved ice. Then you would just fill it up with alcohol.

Kevin, the bar manager, would always have a drink going and he wasn't shy about asking anyone else if they wanted one. At the end of the night, I wondered how Kevin found his way home. The food and beverage manager would come by and pour himself a stiff one, too. If I worked out of the main bar near the dining room, I was the cocktail waiter. Most of the time, though, I would be working downstairs where I would make the drinks for the members in the reading room. This was the first place where I did some waiting on tables as well.

Working there I wasn't making enough money, so guess where I ended up again? That's right: the 5444 Disco I had left just several months earlier. Of course, this time I followed the price list. It was a whole new staff there managed by someone else. I worked two to three evenings a week there.

After a few months at the dumpy apartment, I moved to the University of Toronto area into a furnished room. It was an upscale area and I was paying a higher rent. The location was perfect, though—right by the subway.

How I Took a Bartending Course and Traveled for Seventeen Years

I was trying to get things going at that time, so I enrolled in a basic food preparation course. I was trying to make ends meet, but ended up dropping out of the course because I couldn't afford it anymore. As it turned out, I was the only one working in the class. The others were collecting unemployment insurance and getting paid to go to school. They continued on.

Later in 1982, I left the Racquet Club to learn how to provide table-side service at another club by the lake called the Boulevard Club. I wanted, at this point, to further my knowledge on the dining room side to make myself more hireable.

The maître d' was a guy from Spain. He talked with a lisp and he was dating one of the waiters in the dining room. I knew that because I used to give them lifts to work and if one was missing, so was the other one.

My drinking by then was really bad, but I could still do the job. I would go up the spiral staircase to the sports bar and grab a beer there and before I descended the stairs I had finished the bottle. If we did dinners, we would freely consume a lot of wine. Every night it was the same thing.

I was learning how to do Caesar salads at the table, table-side cooking the Chateaubriand, and lighting up those special coffees. It was fun, and I thought this might be a good place to stay a while.

Then one night the drinking caught up with me. I was assigned to do this dinner with another waiter and we were in charge of the head table. There were a lot of big shots there. The mayor of Toronto and the Federal Energy Minister were present. We were serving Mommessin Export, a red wine from France.

There were television people there and interviews and long speeches. The country was in a crisis. The government of the day were nationalizing the energy sector and they had just put in wage and price controls, which they campaigned against only a year earlier. Unemployment was creeping higher.

While the speeches were going on, this Polish waiter and I start drinking the red wine. I mean, not sipping it, but it was like a contest to see who could drink the most. Then the speeches were over and the guests left.

Ready to head home, the maître d' said he was real pleased with everyone's work and invited us to stay for a drink. Everyone agreed it would be a good way to finish off the night, so we attacked the liqueur trolley.

After a couple of belts of Grand Marnier, I started throwing up. It was like a switch had been turned off. I didn't know who I was. Sicker than a dog, I couldn't drive home. The maître d' offered to take a cab home with me. I arrived at my place and he asked if he could come in. Knowing what his motive might have been, I was at least sober enough to say no, that I would be fine. I got out of the taxi. It was -10 degrees Celsius outside. I got to the door and I didn't have my keys. They were at work!

There I was, wearing a vinyl leather jacket with a zipper that didn't work. You know how vinyl reacts to cold? It just captures the cold and holds it. I had to walk three to four miles to work to get my keys and wallet.

I got to the door and saw the night cleaner. "Great," I thought, "someone to let me in." But this guy pretends he doesn't know me and would not open the door! I looked in the parking lot and my car was sitting right there. I couldn't even get into it.

Recalling where the Polish waiter lived, I walked on the bridge overlooking the railway tracks and highway heading to his place. I knocked, and his wife screamed at me, telling me he was asleep and to get lost. What do I do next?

Well, I did what any homeless person would do. I found myself a donut shop to spend the night. I remember the owner trying to shoo me away, but after I tried to explain what had happened, he relented and gave me a coffee. I laid my head on the counter till the sun came up.

At the crack of dawn I walked to the club, where I found my keys and wallet on a table in the banquet hall. I drove home and got into a warm bath and called work later on to see if I could get that night off. I was scheduled to start at 4. They said no, that I had to come in. So I worked that night.

Looking back, I have to say what transpired seemed strange. Up to that time, I knew my limits. I could drink a lot, but I knew when to quit. But that night a line was crossed. I stopped drinking at work for quite a while after that night.

My three months probation was coming up and I was due for a raise. The maître d' suggested we all go to a nightclub. So that night we all went to a bar downtown called Mushrooms. I discovered that everyone I worked with was digging members of the same sex. The raise was never brought up. I never saw any of them again after that, and a couple of days later I had my job back at the Racquet Club.

I moved again shortly thereafter to the North of Toronto into another room, hoping to save some money. It was the winter of 1982-83.

During 1982 a lot had happened. Three moves and several jobs, two of which I returned to after leaving. The move to Toronto was a major disappointment. It was a difficult time, so I began to look for a new beginning.

Looking for a New Beginning

After the experiences of 1982 and especially after the night spent in the donut shop, I wanted to make the following year much better. I began to like what I was doing a lot more, probably because I was gaining some confidence and getting good. I liked the action behind the bar too. But Toronto was lacking in something. Maybe I was a displaced Quebecer who would have rather stayed in Montreal than move away from it.

I liked to travel. I had taken that trip to Europe when I was 18 years of age, thanks in large part to my stepfather who worked for Air Canada. The fact that I could fly standby anywhere with the airline gave me the opportunity to see different places.

Going to Europe for 45 days was a great experience. Hawaii and California when I was 16 years old and the numerous trips to Florida to escape the winters were fun too. After the trip to Europe, I flew to Vancouver and traveled around there and the Rockies. Then I flew down East to Prince Edward Island and Nova Scotia. I hitchhiked the way back from Sydney, Nova Scotia to Toronto. There were also trips I took with my Dad and his new family. A Caribbean cruise and a trip to Myrtle Beach, South Carolina come to mind right away.

So that made me the adventurous kind, always ready to try something new. That could explain the number of jobs and moves I made in those early years.Maybe I was in the right occupation but in the wrong place up to that time.

My financial situation at the beginning of 1983 was not very good. I was back at the Racquet Club and not making great money. There were no tips. Learning to budget for two weeks between pay cheques was difficult to do after getting tips every night.

Things were also getting expensive. I had a car that was parked most of the time. What was the point of having it if I used public transit? When the car insurance was coming up to be renewed, I looked at what it was going to cost me for the year and what I had in my bank account. Usually, I had enough to pay it off in one shot. Now it looked like I had to pay it monthly.

Here I was in Toronto, supposed to be having a good time. Sure, I was single, but I didn't have much money to enjoy the city. I had no assets at all, a furnished room, an older car, and no girlfriend.

You know for a few years I thought I was the only person who was single and 23 who lived like that. But as time passed, I realize that many people live the same way. It is no coincidence. Relatives and acquaintances may think you are living the jet set life, but really you are just trying to make ends meet.

Everything I did would be on the inexpensive side. It was still fun, though. Free outdoor concerts at Ontario Place in the summer. I recall seeing Neil Sedaka and Aretha Franklin perform there. I was always going to the football game, a museum, or by the waterfront to be amongst the crowds. I soaked up what I could living in Toronto. The Toronto Islands you catch by ferry were nice too.

I did meet a few girls but no one to make me stay in one spot. I was far from being settled. I just wanted to do something different. I thought of moving out of the province. My job continuity was not good either. A fresh start somewhere else would be beneficial.

That is when I opened up the Globe and Mail newspaper and saw an ad that was looking for a headwaiter to work at this resort on the Banff - Jasper Highway located in the Rocky Mountains on the Alberta side.

My resume was fixed up to show a bit of job stability and personal growth. I mailed it out and pretty much forgot about it. You see, the Globe and Mail is a national newspaper, so this ad was going out nationwide. What were the chances?

About ten days later I got a call. Bernard was on the other end of the phone and asked me if I still wanted the job. I emphatically said yes and he asked if I could report there a couple of weeks before May long weekend. "Of course!"

It was April and not a problem. I was living out of a furnished room and paying weekly rent so that was not a big deal. My worldly possessions consisted of two suitcases and a carry-on bag. I sold the car and saved on the insurance.

I phoned my relatives to tell them I was heading out west. It was a seasonal summer job, I explained, and I would be back after the season was over. But really, I was pretty through with Toronto at that point. It was time to move onto other experiences.

Getting final instructions on how to get there, I bought my plane ticket for Calgary and prepared myself for the new adventure.

The Beautiful Canadian Rockies

The place was the Saskatchewan River Crossing, and it was situated midway between Banff and Jasper, Alberta on the Icefields Parkway. This was going to be my summer employment and my escape from the city of Toronto.

I flew into Calgary then took a two and a half hour bus ride to Banff where I checked into a hotel for the night. I rested up that night for the Brewster Tour Bus that would take me to my new job as head waiter. As soon as I got to Banff, I totally fell in love with the mountains and the clean air. The total scene there was so different from living in a hustle-bustle city like Toronto. "I could totally get into this," I thought. "What an adventure!"

Banff is a tourist destination to begin with, so naturally all the service people that worked in the restaurants and bars were very friendly. It seemed too that the people who frequented the local eateries were a lot more patient. Since most of them were on holiday, they were pretty relaxed. That was the first impression I got. "This gig at the Crossing should be a blast," I thought.

During the bus ride up there, we stopped at Moraine Lake and Peyto Lake. The water is a beautiful blue color that is attributed to the snow from the mountains and glacial deposits. I thought to myself, "what an experience to see this when only a month ago I was contemplating how to pay for my car insurance."

The Saskatchewan River Crossing was a family-run operation built from scratch and it was a busy spot. It had an inn, a couple of restaurants, a gift shop that did mountains of business, and a gas station, which came in handy, as it was the only one on the entire Parkway between Banff and Jasper. There was the one restaurant for the bus tours and the other one where I was going to work. Overnight guests of the hotel and others passing through who didn't want cafeteria food were the people I would be serving.

It was as fine dining as you would expect situated where it was in the middle of the mountains. We had a full stock of liquor and a pretty good wine list. Also, at the table we presented the fish on a platter (sole or the trout I recall) and filleted it right there as part of the presentation.

I arrived at noon and met Bernard who was from Montreal. He was the dining room manager and had worked there for a couple of years already. He stayed year-round. He talked many times of how quiet the winters were as the Parkway, for the most part, was closed due to the heavy snow. He made it known that this was probably going to be his last year and then he would be heading back to Montreal. After a short time there I could understand why he might want to head back to the city.

You see, back in 1983, for those of you who can't remember that far back, there were not the lines of communication that we have now. The only television channel we could get at the time at this isolated location in the mountains was the Turner Broadcast Network out of Atlanta. I guess they had a satellite to beam the signals up to us. So all I could see all year were Atlanta Braves baseball games.

To phone the Crossing you had to have a radio operator connect your call, which was pretty expensive, so I never phoned anyone. I used to save that for when I went on that noon tour bus ride that went north to Jasper. I would stay overnight in Jasper just to get out and make all my calls there, and then grab the same tour bus back early the next morning.

I shared a room with three others and every night there would be a chat with the others and a few drinks shared. What else do you do when you are in such a spot? In fact, that was the only time I ever bonged a beer. You take this funnel and you pour the bottle of beer in it while twisting the bottom of it to keep the beer from flowing down. Then, when it is full, you open the mouth and untwist the tube and wham the beer goes into your mouth in a few seconds. I did it once and that was enough.

Now all of us know shooters like B52s nowadays, but it was around this time that shooters were just becoming known. In the early 80s someone in Edmonton started this craze and of course the industry hasn't looked back since. So, on our one day off a week, we would eat in the dining room and have a meal and order all kinds of shooters. The weather in the mountains being so unpredictable, what could one do? It even snowed in July!

The summer went by quickly. It was mainly work and, with the exception of the odd lunch barbeque, my work took place in the evening. That left the day to explore. I took the tour of the Columbian Icefields and walked on the glacier.

I remember going for hikes on the trails. One experience that I had while hiking was encountering a goat. I thought, "no problem, it will step aside and let me pass." The goat started walking toward me and, before I knew it, there were about fifteen goats following it. I stood there for a second then started quickly walking backwards. They started to pick up speed as well. Pretty soon, I was running and they were running. Was I going to be attacked by a bunch of goats!! They chased me all the way to the lodging before they turned off. I told this story to the others and, to them, I was just one big city slicker. They laughed and laughed.

But animals in the wild act a whole lot different than seeing them in a zoo. In the wild, you are the trespasser. The experience of that and just being one with nature was all new to me. Could I get used to working here?

I even started to eat natural foods such as yoghourt with almonds and honey. Fast foods were a thing of the past. I was getting the fresh air now, instead of the smog from the city.

I worked with some interesting people. One of my roommates from Montreal talked of what he was going to do after the summer, which was to work with a circus troupe that went on to be better known as the Cirque de Soleil.

The waiting on tables was pretty fun. I found that dealing with people on holiday was a lot easier to handle. Everyone was from somewhere else, so I got a chance to converse and learn from other's experiences.

In the end, though, the isolation was a bit much and I started to miss the privacy of living on my own. Living with others was not something I had been used to before this and the quarters were pretty tight. There was no escaping others.

So in the middle of August I headed back east feeling that the summer whirlwind experience got a lot out of my system. I was ready to finally settle and stay somewhere for a while. After all, I was 24 years of age by then.

Enough of the running around. Get a nice apartment for a change. Cook a meal for once. Get a girlfriend. But where, was the question.

Finding Success in Montreal

I wanted to try my luck finding a job in Montreal again and not head back to Toronto. I wanted to return to my roots, you could say.

Making my intent known before I left, Bernard, who still had a couple of months to go before he was to return to Montreal, graciously gave me the keys to his apartment so I had a place to crash. This gave me a chance to look for work and my own place.

I really liked the location of the apartment. It was in the heart of the city in the university section. There was still some warm weather left and I spent a lot of the time reacquainting myself with the joie de vivre of this French metropolis.

As Bernard's return approached, I still had not found a job. One thing that didn't change over the past three years was you had to learn the French language in order to work in the industry. I didn't know it well enough, but if I ever did find a job, I wanted to take a course and learn it.

As luck would have it, and just in time, I did find a job. It was toward the end of September and it was a place on the West Island in Pointe Claire, which was one of the places where English was still widely spoken.

The restaurant was called Marilyn's Hamburgers. Yes, I was going to sell hamburgers and fries with gravy! Now, in the list of all the places I have ever worked this one ranks way down there. What do you do when you need a job? Take anything!

The owner of Marilyn's was a member of a motorcycle gang. He or another guy would cook the burgers and fries. He would rarely show his face in the restaurant. He would sit in the kitchen in his motorcycle jeans and leather jacket equipped with a chain around his waist. On the heavy side, he scared the living daylights out of me. Intimidating is a good word to describe his character.

I was the bartender, waiter, and host. When you took the order, you were expected to remember the entire order by heart. The result was you would run like crazy to the kitchen and verbalize the order before you forgot it. Not an easy thing to do when it was a six-top you were taking the order from.

How many ways can you garnish a burger! The hamburger did not come with a bun either, but with toasted bread. It was a place people would travel miles for a taste of this burger. Now, the proprietor being of the motorcycle gang variety, you can imagine what the tips were like working in this place.

Anyway, when taking the order you would ask if they wanted white or brown bread toasted. Also, back in those days you had to ask how they liked the burger cooked. Then ask if they wanted cheese with it. Then you would get everyone telling you what they wanted on the burger. "I will have mine with fried onions, or sautéed mushrooms, no pickle, hold the mustard, with barbeque sauce. What about the bacon? No relish, and can I have my fries with gravy? Or add the curd cheese for poutine."

C'mon already!! Then I would have to tell the kitchen and they would cook those burgers up like there was no tomorrow. When you heard the bell you would run like crazy or risk being yelled at to come and pick up those burgers.

Then you would get their Pepsi, beers, or shots and deliver them and greet the next table and do the same thing over again. It was like basic training for waiters!

The fun part began when the table asked for separate bills. Our cash register was just that. I think it was one of the first ones ever built. Even back in 1983, this model was an antique. No memory or anything. So you had to remember what each individual had to eat and punch it up there and then. I have to admit, I had to cheat a bit and write some stuff down so I could remember what everyone had when it got busy and it came time for them to pay.

The bar was open till 2:30 in the morning and I recall some long nights serving two other people drinks at the bar till the wee hours. It was brutal. I didn't like this place at all. But it kept me in Montreal and I guess if Marilyn's did not hire me who knows where I would have ended up.

Meanwhile, I found my own apartment in NDG, just outside of Montreal. It was a dandy apartment. I bought some furnishings on my credit card. I had a nice front room, kitchen, and bedroom with a balcony. I was livin' the dream.

The only thing that needed changing at this point was Marilyn's Hamburgers. Besides, I was not sure how it would do in the cold winter months that were coming up soon. I had to get out of there somehow.

It was December of 1983 when I checked out this ad in the evening newspaper. A private club was looking for a bar manager. It asked that applicants apply and send their resume to the post office box provided. Wow, how times have changed. Remember sending resumes to a post office box?

Anyway, it had no mention of needing to know French, so I tweaked my resume and sent it in. About ten days later I received a call from Dave to come in for an interview. Dave was the club general manager.

We hit it off immediately. He explained that the present bar manager was getting fired. He wasn't happy with his performance and he needed someone who was reliable and trustworthy. I was their guy.

It was the University Club of Montreal. Just south of McGill College, it had been around for quite a long time. One of the co-builders of this club was none other than Stephen Leacock, a famous Canadian author. The club had an exclusive members list ranging from well-know politicians to bankers to leaders in just about every industry of the day.

As the bar manager, I was in charge of inventory, ordering everything for the bar, and keeping our wine cellars organized. It was quite an extensive wine list. Before wines came into fashion, Dave's wine cellar was way ahead of its time.

It was a time of celebration for me. I was leaving Marilyn's Hamburgers to take on a job that meant something for the first time. I was going to be a bar manager.

So, on February 1st 1984, I started at the University Club of Montreal. It was six days before my 25th birthday. It was indeed a great gift and an opportunity to settle back in Montreal again!

1984 – 1987

Settling In

With great excitement I started my new job as bar manager of the University Club of Montreal. A private club that specialized in wine tasting and gourmet dinners, this was a great spot to learn about food and beverage. The chef from France even had us eat pigeon numerous times for our staff meal. I never became a great fan of pigeon, but in France they are considered a delicacy.

The two and a half years I worked there I learned a lot about inventory control. We had a wine list of over 150 wines and plenty more in storage that the club manager was going to make available over time. He was one who would buy wines to lay down for a couple of years to age before releasing.

We worked together to expand the wine cellar. I introduced a perpetual inventory system whereby at the end of each month I would photocopy the inventory. Every day I would subtract the bottles we'd used the previous day. It was handy to have this on hand. When the manager called and wanted to know how much of a particular vintage we had left, I would just look it up on the list.

Of course, when I had to place an order for beer, wine, or liquor it was easy to do as well, having this system. The functions for the following week would come to me and I would order what we needed. It was pretty easy and I was a stickler on getting the inventory right.

Also, I had this older French gentlemen working during the evening when I was home. When I arrived in the morning I would check to see that what was used and what he requisitioned were one and the same. On the odd occasion when we had big dinners and there were cases of wine consumed I would double check to see that everything was correct. Occasionally, I would find he missed charging a case of wine when I did a quick count the next morning. So, for finding mistakes it was beneficial. That list was like gold.

When I said 'at home in the evening,' you heard correctly. My hours were 10:30 to 6:00 Monday to Friday. Holidays I had off and the club closed for three weeks during the summer. I could work overtime when they needed me. Usually, it was a special dinner and I was used to pour some wine. On other occasions, I would work a portable bar for a function.

The bar was enclosed. In other words, I was the service bartender for two waiters at lunch on the main floor and I received the drink orders for the other two floors via a dumbwaiter. The waiter would hang the drink order on a clothes peg in the elevator. They would ring the bell and I would wait at the bar to grab the order. Then I'd make the drinks and send the elevator hurtling back to where it came from with drinks in tow.

At busy times that bell would be ringing like crazy and if you didn't get to the dumbwaiter quick enough, it would be soon gone back up to a waiting waiter with another drink order.

At the club, members used to need someone to do in-house catering for them. Usually a waitress and I would head to their place with the food and alcohol. While they entertained the guests, I would be tending bar and the other would be passing around canapés and hors d'oeuvres. We would get paid cash. Usually we got paid about $25-$30 an hour. Not bad on top of what I was making.

One of those parties I did was for Prime Minister Trudeau. He left politics in 1983. At the time, he was joining the Blaikie Law Firm in Montreal and it was at Mr. Blaikie's house that the former prime minister was going to be a guest. We heard the news that he was joining the law firm even before the public got wind of it. Quite a nice guy, he just ordered a Perrier when he arrived. I didn't think I was going to see him get drunk or anything, but that would have made for a much more memorable evening!

The two waiters I made drinks for during lunch were hilarious. All we did all lunch hour was tell jokes. One of the waiters was Jamie and this guy had an amazing repertoire of jokes. He would have us bent over laughing so hard. Some of his jokes I still remember to this day.

Meanwhile, I was enjoying my nifty apartment as well. It was huge compared to the other places I used to live in and I spent a large amount of time just chilling out. I don't know whether it was because I was running around for the few years before, but I was feeling pretty settled in my new surroundings.

I loved living in Montreal and was glad to be back. I had finally found a job, which I figured, at the time, I could probably spend a lifetime at with no problem. After the first year they gave me a 15% raise. The bar cost was great. Everyone and I got along well. The second year I did an even better job and got a 7.5% raise. I think you know where I am heading with this one.

During my vacation in the summer of 1985, I went to this super club for a week in Jamaica. It was called Hedonism. It had just started up, so I thought I would check it out. Quite the spot, I went parasailing and did a few other things.

I also made a decision to improve myself and take a home study course in hotel, motel and restaurant management. Rather than go to bars now on a Saturday night I would spend my time at the kitchen table writing feverishly, trying to finish my assignment so I could mail it in and start the next chapter. It was a time of personal development for me. It took just over two years to complete the course. What I thought would come of this course I wasn't sure, but I definitely did not want it to go to waste.

It was around my 27th birthday when I completed the course. I had just received half the raise I'd been given the year before. Slowly, I began to realize that perhaps I had reached my full potential there. Fernando, the maître d', was an icon and was going to be there for a long time to come.

I didn't really make a whole bunch of new friends. I dated a few girls, but most of the time I was just chasing them with no real luck. I never was in the bar scene even though I worked in plenty of them. I was socially awkward you could say.

I would take the same bus and subway to and from work and through familiarity I would meet girls that way. Where I worked there was no one special. So basically, by the spring of 1986, I was looking to do something else. I was getting the itch.

At some point I just thought, like the song says, *is that all there is*? I mean, for some, my lifestyle was ideal. But I kept thinking that I was going to find someone, get married, work my ass off, retire, and that would be it. Oh yeah, have a couple of kids too. The question always was, what else would I like to do before all that happened?

So, in May of 1986, I started my job search once again. But this time something a bit more exciting was what I was looking for.

A Big Change

It was May of 1986 and coming up to a couple of months short of two and a half years that I was working at the University Club as a bar manager. Things were going swell and I was settling in after having moved about for quite some time before. Still though, after having completed my hotel restaurant management home study course, I really wanted to do something exciting with what I'd just learned. I felt I wasn't quite ready to settle down just yet either.

So I started to work on my resume by outlining not only my work experience the past couple of years, but also highlighting my completed course. I thought about what I would like to do and it occurred to me that the cruise ship industry was gaining popularity. The popular show of the day was entitled *Love Boat*. "How enjoyable would it be to work on a cruise ship," I thought. Everyone started talking about going on a cruise or working on one.

I decided I wanted to give it a shot. I went to a travel agency and asked to see their travel guide to copy down all the cruise ship company addresses in Florida and on the West Coast. This was the quickest way of getting contact addresses and sending out a resume at the time. Don't forget, the Internet was still not around then.

I sent out a half dozen resumes to different cruise ship companies in June, applying for bartending positions. Holland America, Norwegian Caribbean Cruises, and Royal Caribbean Cruise Line were my top choices and the most popular at the time. Sitmar Cruises out of Los Angeles was another.

I didn't know what to expect. I was sure many other people would be competing for the same job. I figured my resume would be put in a pile with the rest of them and someday someone would go through them and put the good ones aside for when an opening came up. I even figured I would have to call back to follow up a few weeks later.

Normally, I wouldn't be putting my work contact number on the resume. I put my home number so they could call and leave a message. I didn't think an employer would go to such great lengths to look up the number where I was working and call me during the day.

The end of June was approaching and my resumes had gone out only a couple of weeks before. I was getting ready to plan my holiday when the club would be closed for three weeks in August. Then the phone rang one day after lunch. Morris at the front desk transferred this call to me. I never got calls at work. I thought it was an emergency.

It was Norwegian Caribbean Lines on the phone! They wanted me to come on board as a bartender. They asked me if I could be in Miami in a week's time. I replied that it was impossible, as I needed to give my notice at work. I didn't want to leave on bad terms.

Finally, we agreed on my getting down there in three weeks time.

I was really excited when I got off the phone. But then what I'd just done hit me. I had to give my notice as quickly as possible, without delay. I woke up that morning with a pretty consistent lifestyle and in one call, I totally turned my life upside down. This was a big move. I was excited and scared at the same time. Was I doing the right thing leaving my comfortable lifestyle?

This was the only time I have ever given notice with tears in my eyes. Dave was very understanding, but he said, "Fernando the maître d' is going to really miss you, and you should tell him." Fernando was Portuguese and one hell of a nice guy and maître d'. I broke the news to him and he couldn't believe it. I guess they thought I was going to stay forever.

Up to that time, I never had grown attached to the people I worked with like I did at the University Club. It has to rate as one of the finest places I have ever worked. Everything ran tickety-boo there.

How I Took a Bartending Course and Traveled for Seventeen Years

During the next three weeks, two of which I spent still working at the club, I had to sublet the apartment, sell my furniture, sell my car, and change my Canadian address to where my Mother lived.

It would be ten years before I owned another car. Eight years before I would have my own address again. Ten years before I would own any furniture.

My Father came to visit me and we had a couple of great days golfing in the Laurentiens and took a boat ride on Lake St. Louis. It was a memorable visit. He had just retired and was enjoying his free time. Unfortunately, it was probably the last good time we had as his health soon started to fail.

I managed to get everything in order and bought my plane ticket for Miami. Arriving a day early, I reserved a hotel room in Key Biscayne on the beach so I could relax a bit. Relaxing was really out of the question, though, as I had to get a chest x-ray and write a bartending exam before embarking on the ship. All I did was take the taxi all over the place. My friend from Montreal who was holidaying in Fort Lauderdale was staying not far away, so he visited me. We went out for a bite to eat and talked about the ships.

That night I didn't sleep well at all. I was apprehensive about what the ship would be like and just exhausted from all the running around I had to do during the three weeks before I left Montreal.

In hindsight, anyone who accepts to just pack up and go anywhere on the drop of a dime should ask a lot more questions than I did to that guy on the phone. I had no idea what I was in for. It sounded exciting though. It was the biggest cruise ship in the world at the time. It was the SS Norway. It carried 2000 passengers and around 800 crewmembers. Formerly known as the SS France when it was commissioned back in 1962. It was an old ship refitted for the cruise industry.

The seven-day voyage would start off in Miami then head to Nassau, St. Thomas, Saint Maarten and the cruise ship's private island.

The duration of the contract was ten months. Yes, ten months! No day off. Just work till you drop. So much for working days only and weekends off. That was a thing of the past now.

The SS Norway

Part 1

There I was in Miami, July, 1986, getting ready to work on the biggest cruise ship in the world at that time.

In early afternoon I was checked in and the purser took my passport. Then I was shown my living quarters down at what seemed like the bottom of the ship. It was deep in the bowels of the ship below water level. There were four of us in that room that was, if I could put it mildly, like a hot-house. No port-hole, just darkness. Someone left their radio on. There was nobody in the room. I was told that I would be working a bar where there was a jazz band playing. That is where everyone headed when the ship began to head out of port.

I took a look at the communal showers. All the guys showered there and the smell of bleach permeated the hot air. I checked out the staff cafeteria and found out that the main diet was fish and rice. Great once or twice a week, but everyday! You got to be kidding! Especially when I noticed who was serving up the food. That person did not add to my appetite when he started putting his fingers up his nose!

Off to the bar I went to start my first shift and, as you might expect, I was ransacked. People were ordering drinks from everywhere. Just after we left port I heard that three crewmembers jumped ship hoping, I guess, to start a new life in America.

Being North American, I was definitely a minority on the ship. Many were from the Philippines and South America. They were all working for a menial wage and long hours. For them, though, it was a lot of money. I had walked into the present-day form of slavery, I thought.

The pay, of course, is what would interest most people who would work under such conditions. That is where the company definitely was not all that upfront. I was to be paid $1500 a month plus 15% of my sales. But only if my 15% added up to over $1500. In other words, if the sales added up over $1500, I would get the difference.

For example, to make more, I would have to sell over $10,000 worth of drinks. If I sold $10,100, that extra 15% of $100 would come to $15. So I would make $1515 for the month.

Now, not all the passengers would drink or frequent my bar, but it seemed reasonable over a month to easily smash by a wide margin $10,000 in sales. There was one caveat. The bartenders would have to work at a bar where they would be serving drinks directly to the guest so they would get credit for the drink sold. But what would happen was the company moved bartenders every week between serving drinks directly to the guests and being stuck in the back making drinks for the cocktail waitresses. Therefore, we would get no credit that second week for sales. The waitresses would get it all. This made the chances slim for bartenders to make more than their $1500 a month. I remember some bartenders who were up till 4 AM in the discotheque working their butts off for nothing because they worked the service bar. It was an unfair system.

The company never really paid out any gratuities to bartenders. If a bartender had high sales heading toward the end of the month, they would stick them at a service bar just to bring their sales back down. No doubt, the cocktail waitresses made a killing. The bartenders worked harder though.

The work was slave-like. I worked in the entertainment lounge from four in the afternoon till about eleven or twelve at night. Then the next morning I was doing bar requisitions and going to the Lido Deck by the pool to spot the bartender there while he took his lunch. That would be between twelve and two usually. Then it was back downstairs and grabbing a quick shower then get ready to open my assigned bar at four.

There was no end.

Seeing some of the bartenders who were already on board for seven to eight months was not a pretty sight. Their character was that of a bunch of people who were so totally exhausted it was like they were running on instinct. Mentally and physically exhausted, all they did was sleep when they had a chance. Shut out from the outside world, they certainly did not offer much in the way of conversation.

I probably worked in an easier bar than they did, but it was still draining. Drinks were ordered by the half-dozen. People would be buying rounds of drinks and all they had to worry about was signing the slip and showing their cabin keys. They would pay at the end of the cruise.

I heartily enjoyed it if someone would just order a beer. I started to not enjoy bartending so much.

For food, I decided that I was not going to eat in the crew mess. But where was I going to get some food I would like? I made a discovery that there was an officer mess. So my plan each day would be to wait till they had finished eating and sneak in there to grab as much as I could to eat. Then I'd get the hell out of there.

There was shrimp cocktail, sandwiches of all kinds, and fresh fruit. I was like a person on the run as I savagely attacked their buffet. Even so, I was losing weight. The ports of call were not that interesting after the first visit. Always having to use the tender was a pain as well. You had to wait till all the passengers disembarked before taking the tender to shore and return quickly before they all started to head back.

I even found myself heading to the passenger decks to use the bathroom. The ones we had were disgusting! So I found a way to sneak in areas where the crew was not allowed and find a public washroom.

Perhaps I should go on to tell you what it was like serving cruise ship passengers. The SS Norway was a ship that was quite affordable to everyone. Therefore, anyone who was on a tight budget took this cruise. Obviously, any profit the SS Norway took in was because of volume and not because of the luxury factor.

When I was bartending in the entertainment lounge, I actually got into a misunderstanding with a guest. He was from Cleveland and I happened to ask him why Cleveland got such a bad rap. I was trying to be empathetic and this guy took it all the wrong way.

I spent a month as a bartender, then they switched me to Sommelier in the dining room. Our sections were about 60 to 70 passengers in size, but the workload was slightly exaggerated. Most tables would have a bottle of wine bought for them by the travel agent and they would sip on it all week. As a sommelier, you were also responsible for serving non-alcoholic and alcoholic beverages and wines of course.

Also, you had your own set of wine glasses. You were assigned racks of wine glasses with your name or initials in black marker scribbled on the rack. At the end of the shift, you had to pay the dishwasher $5 so he would clean your glasses and put them away for you in the wine glass room. There were times you would head into dinner for the first seating and you would be short a couple of racks, so you had to steal from other people's racks. It was real mafia-like working with these dishwashers. They made sure they got your money and even then what they promised wasn't always delivered.

I was happier working as a sommelier, though, because at the end of the shift at least I ate one square meal. As a sommelier, I had to work the midnight buffet and be up in the morning to do the requisitions.

One Saturday morning before the beginning of the next cruise, all the sommeliers had to change the wine cellar. A complete revamp of the wine list was done with the new one beginning that evening. We finished about 15 minutes before our 6:00 dinner service. Fortunately, I had a group of bible thumpers who didn't drink at that first sitting. Didn't make any money, but it was better than running around that night. I don't think I even had time to shower before service.

Some of the requests from passengers were crazy. Mid-way through a cruise, the wine manager approached me to ask if I could take over this table in my co-worker's section. "Sure," I said, wondering what problem he could have been having with the table. Well, you see, this family wanted to be served first out of 500 people when they got to the dining room. If you can imagine the doors opening at 6:00 and a huge swarm of people rushing to their assigned tables all at once. In order for this table to be served first, they had to be the first to enter, first to sit down, first to order and even then the sommelier had to find his way to the bar and be first in line. This was all impossible to achieve.

So I introduced myself and asked what they would like tomorrow night. Taken a bit aback, they gave their order of a beer, two Shirley temples for the kids and a soda. Next night at 5:55 I went to the bar and ordered their drinks. The bartender laughed and said, "we aren't even open yet."

I retorted back, "I know what I am doing." I got the drinks and dropped them off at their table.

The doors opened and the dining room began to fill up. No sign of my table who wanted to be served first. Finally, about 6:15, they came sauntering in. By this time, the beer bottle is covered in condensation and the ice had melted in the other drinks. They asked me what was going on. I told them, "these are the drinks you ordered last night for tonight. You were not here when we opened, but I can assure you that you were the first served in the entire dining room as you requested tonight."

Their reply was simply to say, "oh yes, that's right." From that moment on, they just told me to forget about them being first. It didn't really matter. Well, at least I got them to stop complaining, but I did notice from that night on a line of sommeliers at the bar before we opened to get a head start on delivering their drinks!

The SS Norway

Part 2

The reason the SS Norway experience is divided into two parts is I couldn't talk about the ship without separating the good from the bad. It is difficult to talk about anything that could be so bad yet so good in the same segment.

Before I left my apartment and life in Montreal, I have to admit that I was becoming a bit of a hermit. I was really settling in and to go on the ship in such short notice was quite the extreme opposite of being settled. Not really leaving anything behind, I was ready for some adventure and on this ship I got it.

It was like going from being a solitary person to a rock star. Up to that time, I'd had to hunt for girls to get a date. All of a sudden, they were throwing themselves at me.

When I worked the bar, there was one cruise when a couple of girls from New York would go to the Cabaret with me after my shift. I would run to my cabin and change into something decent and head to see a show with them. They were buying me the champagne and everything. When they got home, they were both sending me letters telling me to visit.

There was another girl on the ship who was in the live entertainment show on board. She was also from the States. Another time, there was a beautiful girl sitting in my section during one cruise. When we were in St. Thomas, she invited me to come meet her during the afternoon at the beach. I remember she was from Cincinnati. So that afternoon I went to the beach and found out she was 16 years of age from her father. Oops! Then I remember one cruise when there were 250 single women from Dallas on board. I wasn't allowed in the discotheque at night as a crewmember, but I got dressed up for it anyway and checked out the scene there. The manager saw me and just let it go.

How I Took a Bartending Course and Traveled for Seventeen Years

Between spending time in the crew bar and working, I was exhausted. One lunch hour I even forgot to show up for my lunch shift. They were looking for me all over the ship and finally caught up with me on the crew sundeck soaking up some rays. Another time, I didn't even bother getting up to do the wine requisition that morning. I was so tired I couldn't even finish writing a postcard before the pen dragged across the card because I had closed my eyes and started to nod off.

As a sommelier, when I was at least assured of getting one good meal a day, the calorie burn and the food intake was a mismatch. I was losing weight and, a tall lanky guy to begin with, it wasn't doing me any good.

One cruise I served the Mamas and the Papas minus Mama Cass, of course, who passed away a few years before. On the last night of their stay, I was invited up to their cabin with a few others. They never played any of their hits, but I remember they played a lot of other songs. Mainly the Beatles. It was a grand time singing along with them and chatting. They also drank Dom Perignon during their meal and took a couple with them up to their room for later on. It greatly increased my sales for the month and I ended up making more money on my gratuities because of it. But compared to the workload, $2000 a month still didn't cut it.

Despite all the hardship, though, the ship taught me one big thing: there is a whole world out there. For the first time, I felt like I was attractive to the opposite sex. I mean, I guess I always was, but being on the ship I met more girls than I had in my lifetime up to that point.

So, that is basically what happened on the SS Norway. Good times and bad. I think if I could have eaten better I could have stuck it out longer. I wasn't always successful sneaking into the Officers' mess to grab the leftovers. I drank more than I ate. That crew bar saw a lot of me after work.

Time To Go

By about the seven-week mark, I was dragging myself around. There was no way I was going to fulfil my 10 month contract. To sum up everything, I couldn't live in the squalid living conditions, the sweat-box of a cabin, and scrounge for food from the officer's mess until that one meal at 11PM in the dining room.

I was even scared I had contracted AIDS at the time. Don't laugh because at this period no one was certain how you got infected. It was all over the news and a relatively new phenomenon, so one wasn't sure if it was possible to get it even by kissing someone. I was a bit paranoid over that.

I was not the only one to find the living and working conditions horrible. I met a Canadian waiter four days into a cruise on the crew deck and asked him how he liked it. He answered back that he was getting off Saturday he hated it so much. I asked him how long he had been on and it had only been four days.

To enter the States and board the ship, I had purchased a return ticket for September 15th. Even if I had no plans on returning on that date I still needed to have a return date on my ticket or I would have been stopped at the border. I had no proof that I was hired on the ship, so I had to act like a tourist. Deciding I was going to get off this hellhole, I told them I wanted off the next cruise, which would have been my eighth. This way I would be able to use my return ticket.

If I had managed to work the entire 10 month contract the company would buy your return ticket.

I remember I closed the crew bar on my last night of the 8th week and my final cruise. After closing the bar, I just sat at the bow of the ship looking at the lights of Miami. The ship used to just sit out there till daybreak, until it got the green light to pull along pier-side.

Finally, disembarking about 1 PM, I checked into the hotel where the crewmembers got a discount. Then, as I had about a week and a half before my flight, I relocated to Fort Lauderdale to get some rest and relaxation before heading home to Montreal.

The irony of the situation was that as soon as I got off the ship I started to think I would like to give it another go with another cruise line. "Perhaps Royal Caribbean was much better," I thought. I had been told it was. Newer ships along with more up-to-date staff accommodations sounded like my cup of tea.

How I Took a Bartending Course and Traveled for Seventeen Years

My plan was to fly back home and then head back to Miami and just apply right at the offices located along the pier. I figured as soon as the ships would be coming into Miami they would need some positions filled right away from last minute change of plans from crewmembers.

So, after being in Montreal for a short time, I booked a one-way flight on Presidential Airways via Washington DC then on to Miami. It was a bold move and a stupid one. Booking a one-way ticket with my stopover in Washington was not pleasant. They took me into a holding area and began throwing questions at me. How long was I going to be in the States for? Was I looking for work? What was my reason for visiting etc.? I replied that I was heading to Royal Caribbean in Miami to take a job that was offered to me as bartender.

They asked me what proof I had and I said they gave me their word. A bold thing to say in front of a US Immigration Official! A big deliberation ensued and one of them walked out to check something.

Returning back, he said the next time I needed a letter from the company to say they were employing me. At the time, they were starting to crack down on the cruise lines for not providing any documentation to new hires coming across the border. Some countries had to have a visa anyway, but in my case, coming from Canada, the border crossing was getting tougher to cross. It was a special discount flight that I wanted to take advantage of at the time to save some cash.

I got to Miami and spent a few days there and changed my mind after it all. Imagine just flying down and going through the hassle of being stopped at the border and questioned then deciding in the end I didn't want to subject myself to further experiences on the sea.

With my tail in between my legs, I flew back home to stay with my Mother for a bit. I was like a fish out of water. Wondering what to do and having no real job prospects in Montreal due to my lack of French, I came up with another idea.

Despite my short work span on the ship, an employer really looked favourably at a candidate with ship experience. The reason being is they know how hard it is to work on a ship. So you must have at least a good work ethic.

I had heard there were a lot of jobs in the New England area of the States. I bought the Boston Globe and there were pages and pages of ads for hotel management opportunities. In fact, places like McDonalds were hiring people for $10 an hour just to keep them. It was not a new idea to check out the US even before the cruise ships, as I would occasionally buy the paper just to gawk at the want ads. I sent some resumes stating my intention of visiting between such and such dates and if they were interested to contact me so we could set something up.

I ended up getting a very interested call from this man from a Hilton in Natick, Massachusetts, about 45 minutes from downtown Boston. We set up a day that I would be there to have an interview.

This time, though, rather than fly, I decided I would rather take the bus from Montreal to Boston. It was a lot less expensive and more of an open-date return ticket.

When we crossed the border, instead of just telling the truth, I just said to the customs official I was going to study law at Harvard. He asked me if I watched a lot of LA Law and I said it was my favourite show. He laughed and stamped my passport.

I got into Boston after going through a few States pretty bleary-eyed. Grabbing a bus, I traveled to Natick where I met this guy in his big office. He talked about how hard it was to find good staff and my role was going to be Mr. Everything. Running the restaurant, hiring and training new staff, having a hand in banquets etc....

We clicked immediately and my job now was to head back home and they were going to get me working at the hotel within eight weeks. I would fill out papers on my end that they would send me and their lawyers would get to work on it. I would have a temporary work visa very shortly.

I was really excited. Then after a few days at home, I began to think of the situation. The rentals were sky high and my salary was not that sky high. However, it was a Hilton and it represented a big step up for me. If I succeeded, who knew what the future would bring.

A few days later, the GM phoned and asked me how everything was coming along. I backed out and told him I had changed my plans. He asked me what had happened and I just said that I was going to give it a go here in Montreal instead. I thanked him for thinking so highly of me and wished him all the best. It was cordial, but I could tell he was somewhat shocked by my change of heart.

Maybe it was too soon after the ship. I felt like the previous four to five months were hectic enough and I wasn't ready for another big move. It was breakneck speed. It was leaving my job after two and a half years, then packing up and going to work on a cruise ship. Then having that end abruptly after two months, then flying back to Miami to check out the ships again, then changing my mind. After changing my mind about going on a ship then going to Boston and changing my mind about working in the States. Well, it all seemed like a whirlwind.

It was coming up to November 1986 now and I thought maybe I should just settle down here in Montreal again. Yes, again, after only leaving four months earlier!

I was soon going to be 27 and I thought about really sinking my teeth into something at home. I had the hospitality home study course under my belt and the cruise ship experience out of my system.

Now was the time to really decide on finding a job in a hotel or fine dining restaurant downtown in the heart of the city. I had done a lot and I felt like it was time to just relax. Everything seemed to be going in that direction until I met this other person who gave me another idea.

While Learning French

I really didn't want to be anywhere else but Montreal. So I finally looked into taking a French course so I could get a good job.

I went to the unemployment office to see if I could collect some money while learning the language. Fortunately, I had accrued enough work weeks from my previous job as bar manager with the University Club that I was entitled to a full year of benefits. I enrolled myself in the French course that was to start in January and last through till June.

I was going to stay with my Mother while I took the course. The course would take place from nine in the morning to three in the afternoon, Monday through Friday. Upon its completion in June, I would be ready to take on a good-paying position anywhere in Montreal.

The school was called Centre Imaculée and it was located in LaSalle Quebec. From where I was staying, it was about a 30-minute bike ride when the weather was good. In the winter it was a three-bus ride. It was set up so there were four classes of French and the same number of English classes, each learning the other language. The fun thing was, as well as class instruction, we did a lot of activities with the students who were learning English.

Among other things, we did bowling together and went on a Maple Syrup trip south of Montreal. It was, I have to say, one of the most enjoyable times I've spent. I was just turning 28 and attending school again made we wish I could just return full-time for longer than just six months.

I immersed myself in the French culture. I listened to French talk radio stations and watched the news in French. I read French newspapers. I even read the Hercules Poirot detective books. I would underline the words I didn't know and look them up. At the beginning, I would be underlining every third or fourth word. Then after a few books, the number would dwindle to just two or three a page.

I met a lot of people from all walks of life. A lot of them were just taking the course so they could collect the unemployment cheque for attending the classes. Many were in a state of transition in their life, but needed to know the other language if their intention was to stay in Quebec.

In 1987, what I remember most about the course were those hour-long lunches sitting by the St. Lawrence River soaking up the sunshine from April on till the end of June. I'd talk with others and try to pick up some French women. One in particular was real interested, but she lived with a guy who she told me she had no interest in.

Funny though, she had no interest in him, but couldn't go out on a date with me. She would phone me on Saturday morning when her boyfriend was out doing the shopping and complain to me. I would say, "okay, let's go out," and she would then say no. She was cute as a button, but I had to tell her just to stop phoning. She was driving me crazy.

The course was going along well and I was becoming pretty proficient at speaking French. I was thinking about starting to apply for jobs downtown.

Then one day, this older chap who wanted to get into labour law told me of exchanges that took place between Canada and other countries that included my field of experience. He said, "Why not check it out?" The international work would give me a jump on others when I returned home.

He suggested Switzerland because they had a great reputation for churning out leaders in the hotel and restaurant industry. With my French I could apply to the French part of Switzerland. With this in mind I applied to this exchange program offered by the Canadian government and was accepted. I had filled out the papers and included my resume. Now it was time to wait for a call.

It was April turning into May and with time running out on the course, I called someone in Ottawa to find out what my chances were on finding work in Switzerland.

What they said left me with very little confidence I would find anything. All they do, they said, is put my name in an industry newspaper. Very few get a call, so he suggested I do my own job search. "Just mention you are accepted in an exchange program and looking for an employer to sponsor you."

All right, there I went back to the travel agent to grab the book and start writing down the addresses of hotels in the French part of Switzerland. I came up with 50 names of hotels and restaurants.

Another thing that was coming up was my Mother's decision to move back to Ontario in July. So that meant I had to move out and find a place of my own. But I didn't want to commit to anything long term until I felt all opportunity to work in Switzerland was exhausted.

Finally, just a couple of weeks before we had to vacate the apartment, I received a contract to sign as a food and beverage manager trainee with the Hotel Eden au Lac in Montreux, Switzerland. Out of 50 resumes mailed out, I received 26 replies. All were no, except Hotel Eden au Lac. The contract was for February 1st to December 15 of 1988.

I found a room on the Lakeshore in Lachine that cost me about forty dollars a week. It was a shared kitchen and bathroom. So all I did from July to January was collect my $450 every two weeks and study French.

Then go out with some friends on the weekend. My routine was reading and listening to French radio talk shows. That was it. I wanted to learn as much French as I could and I had the time to do it.

In October I went to the Swiss Consulate downtown and got the work permit stamped in my passport. In November I bought my airplane ticket with KLM. The flight took me to Amsterdam where I was going to meet up with a friend I met on the SS Norway and spend a week touring the Netherlands. No stress. Just get paid to learn and when the money stopped coming in, fly to Europe where I hadn't been since 1977.

So the question you may ask is why I didn't ever settle in Montreal. Probably because it wasn't as I imagined. I finally came to the realization that you can't go back. It had taken a decade to figure it out. If I hadn't left early on with my parents and moved to Ontario, perhaps I would have learned French earlier and stayed.

All I can say is, taking this French course initially to stay in Montreal got me to Switzerland along with the hotel restaurant home study course. I had to have the diploma as well and not just the language.

Funny how you can talk to someone and all of a sudden your life takes on a totally new direction. The moment I got the job in Switzerland, my life became very different. Nothing much was normal after the French course.

The Netherlands

I used my full year of unemployment benefits before heading to Switzerland. It was perfect as they were set to expire at the end of December and I would be flying out in January.

It was a great time: learning French and living on relatively nothing for all that time. The room I was renting was inexpensive and I ate very cheaply. My worldly possessions consisted of a transistor radio, some books, and clothes including my black pants and white shirts for work. Packing was not going to be a problem.

I spent Christmas with my Dad and family in Toronto. My Dad was suffering a lot with his arthritis and he didn't look good at all. My half-brothers were in their teens at this point. We all had a good time. I visited my Mom and other brother, and basically said my goodbyes. I was excited to go to Switzerland, but I really didn't know what to expect other than an incredible opportunity.

I flew to Amsterdam on KLM and landed early in the morning. It was January 1988 and when my friend picked me up at the airport we went for a coffee. It was nine in the morning and still dark. The only other time I had been in Europe was in the summer. I didn't realize how far north Amsterdam was on the map.

We headed to his brother's place where I met his girlfriend. She was quite the gal, with pierced earrings in a lot of places. The next day we headed to Nijmegen near the German border where his parents lived.

I will recap my trip to the Netherlands this way. All I can recall is I drank most of the week I was there and went to different nightclubs. In this university town called Hengelo, I remember my friend taking me to a club at 3:30 AM and there was a line of people at the door waiting to get in. The nightlife in the Netherlands made Montreal look like a convent. It was quite the culture shock.

A couple of other things I remember was most of the towns in Dutch meant a kind of animal in English. One time we were taking the train and each stop translated would be deer or some other animal.

How I Took a Bartending Course and Traveled for Seventeen Years

The other noteworthy experience I remember vividly was, where I slept, I was within earshot of the banging sessions my friend and his girl were having nearby in the next room. Then one morning he had to go to work and said to me his girl was mine for the day if I chose and that she wouldn't mind. I replied back with a big okay, but I couldn't do it. It was a nice gesture, though. Instead, we just went out for the day.

After that week in the Netherlands, I never kept in touch with my friend again. I think he headed back to the ships. It's funny how you come across different people in your life and see them once and even visit them then never hear or see them again afterwards. Back then, if you were too busy to write a letter, it was difficult to stay in touch with anyone. How unlike nowadays when you have instant messaging.

From Amsterdam I flew to Geneva where, upon arrival, I took the mandatory chest x-ray that all foreign workers had to take. I checked into the youth hostel for a week so I could do some touring and check out where I was going to work.

My money was running out, so spending money sightseeing was out of the question in expensive Switzerland. But spending time just walking around and enjoying the mild weather was good enough for me. Situated on the French Riviera with France on the other side of Lake Geneva, I couldn't believe how lucky I was. Not only would I be able to travel around this beautiful part of the world, but I would be getting paid while I was doing it.

In Geneva, I had about 5 days before I was to report to work at the hotel. Only having seen the hotel from a brochure they sent to me, I was anxious to take the train trip to Montreux to check it out.

It was about a 50-minute ride and it travelled right along the edge of the lake. The best way to see the countryside in Switzerland is to take the train. You can set your watch to the trains there as they arrive on time every time. If the train is late, you can see the people starting to get stressed out on the platform. I laugh at that because in Canada you are surprised when any form of transportation is on time.

I got off the train in Montreux and walked to the address where the Hotel Eden au Lac was located. I just stood there and my jaw dropped. You couldn't find a better spot and nicer-looking hotel to work at. I started to get a bit worried about whether my French would be good enough and if they would like me. I was a bit anxious and excited at the same time.

I reviewed all the French I knew over the next few days and reread my *Classical French Cooking* book by Pauli, a well-known Swiss chef, for the third time. I was getting pretty pumped up about the Hotel Eden au Lac. "Let the adventure begin," I thought.

Switzerland 1988 – 89

On February 1st, 1988, I arrived at the Hotel Eden au Lac in Montreux Switzerland to begin work for the next ten and a half months. The hotel was top class and was situated right on the boardwalk of Lake Geneva directly beside the casino where the world famous Montreux Jazz Festival takes place every year.

I was given my own room on the main floor behind some closed doors that, when opened, took you right into the lobby of the hotel. So each morning when I headed to work it was like a grand entrance, you could say. One minute I was showering and the next I was behind a desk right beside my boss, who went by the name of Mr. S. He was the right-hand person of the hotel and took care of its entire operations alongside the hotel directors.

One of the first things I found out was I needed to type up the menus each day for the people who were staying at the hotel who were on the meal plan. "Huh?" I remember saying as I was being shown the typewriter. I didn't know how to type, let alone in French.

The reply I got was, "you don't know how to type, so then you must go to school to learn." Immediately, I was enrolled into a local school called École Blanc to begin a typing course. I learned how to type, not on an English keyboard, but on a French one.

The duties I had were numerous, to say the least. One such duty was ordering the croissants, petit pain, brioche, pain au chocolat and other breads for our breakfast buffet in the morning. Usually, I would order, for example one and a half croissant per person. So, if there were 50 people staying overnight, I would order 75 croissants. Arriving at work in the morning at eight, my duty was to check on how the breakfast service was going, and especially the buffet to see if we were running out of items. Around ten I would notice that we still had some people to arrive, but that we were very low on the croissants. At this point, I would literally run to the local Boulanger and buy more to get us through the breakfast. It would have been horrendous and shameful to have to say to someone that we had no more croissants!!

My duties did not stop there. Breakfast was just one of them. While breakfast was going on, I would be in the store-room filling out the daily requisitions for the bar and kitchen. During the morning, deliveries would arrive from soft drinks, beer and wine, all of which I was responsible for purchasing.

Then we had the big banquet room and some smaller rooms that were used for meetings and conferences. Mr. S would help me with the big tables and afterwards leave me to set up the tables with the notepads and selection of mineral waters. Overhead projectors and screens were put in place with the electrical cords all taped down to the rug so no one would trip over them walking through the room. Usually, he and I would be on hand to greet the convener in the morning to see if any last minute request had to be fulfilled.

At that point, the coffee break times would be confirmed and I would be responsible for setting up the coffee station for the guests, which sometimes numbered over a hundred people. Then at lunch, when they would break, I would scurry into the room and clean away the empty bottles and replenish them. I'd take away any dirty glasses and wipe down any messes left behind.

If that was done, then I would go and check our à la carte restaurant at lunch and see if I could help out anywhere. Sometimes, it would be to take an order from a table or just to run some food. It was a busy spot and with the sun shining most of the time, the outdoor terrace was always busy.

Nowadays here in North America, you find management cocooned in the office doing some useless paperwork during service hours. Well, in Switzerland it is very much a hands-on approach to getting the job done. A manager wearing the suit is expected to be available to help out during busy restaurant hours in Switzerland. If you have to help out and make drinks or run food, you do. You also take food orders from tables, if necessary. It is all about the service. I find too many times the managers disappear when the service happens these days. "Oh." they say, "I am making the schedule," or some other excuse. Then the waiter who is busy running around laments, "Where is the manager?"

For example, I could be finished cleaning and restocking the mineral water in the conference room at lunch when I would be immediately off to the dining room. Or the kitchen might run out of a dry food ingredient and I would be running to the cellar to get it for them. Sometimes I would even run to the store to purchase something on the fly. "Hey, Steven, run to the store and get some polenta!"

You see, if the kitchen had to say they were out of something that would be totally unacceptable. In Switzerland, perfection is a requirement. There are no mistakes allowed and I can recall there were a few times when I was told how to do something and if it wasn't done exactly as I was told, they would tell me till I got it right. Perhaps that is why I am a bit anal now when it comes to detail.

There was one room and it was called the Belle Époque and the furniture was placed just so with a table with a vase on it and a lounge chair facing a certain way. Well, there were times the furniture had to be removed so that a couple of tables could be set up with chairs and mineral water. The overhead projector and screen was placed for a meeting that was about to occur. When the meeting was done, all the equipment and tables were taken away and the furniture that was there before had to be returned. I would put it back in a way that I thought was the exact same place it was before I moved it. The hotel manager would come around and check and tell me the vase was not exactly where it should be. He may have moved it a couple of centimeters from where I put it. Such was the attention to detail that I learned to work with. In essence I became like them.

I learned how to type the function sheets and table d'hôte menus in French. I really learned how to manage my time efficiently.

There were times when I had to take deliveries, fill out requisitions, purchase wines, beers, and soft drinks. Also, I communicated with housekeeping and ordered cleaning supplies. I did the coffee stations and served it to the conference guests and cleaned up afterwards. I worked banquets and was the maître d' for the table d'hôte service in the dining room. Especially when the regular maître d' went on holiday and I had to do it three weeks in a row.

Then, along with all that was counting the inventory at the end of the month and entering it in the computer.

I remember one day in December I started my usual time at 8 AM and worked right through till 2:30 the next morning because I was a bartender for this function that lasted till the wee hours. Mr. S was very kind. He told me I didn't have to come in till ten the next morning! What was that, 18 ½ hours!! Oh, maybe I got a couple of hours in the afternoon off.

I was even a bellboy for Prince Philip when he came for this event with the World Wildlife Federation that took place at the hotel. They told me to grab his bags and take them to his room on the 3rd floor. I served him a beer later that night.

I worked my butt off in Switzerland, but I also partied hard as well. I would start work at eight then finish around seven and head out to the bars in town. I'd stay till close, which wasn't that late, really. I'd be back by one then be up and ready to go the next day.

I took the whole experience in. I was honing my skills in Food and Beverage, especially in classical French Cuisine. I was becoming a real professional in both work ethic and conversing in the French language. I was becoming, you could say, a real dynamo. They called me the Crazy Canuck, I guess because in Switzerland downhill skiing is big and at that time our skiers were called crazy canucks because they were winning races a lot during this time. My nickname came because I would work 10-12 hours, then head out to the bars at night. Well, I only lived in a room, so what was I supposed to do?

When the Jazz Festival came to town there were a lot of stars who stayed at the hotel. One of them was the group Madness, who recorded "Our

House." A big song in the mid-eighties. One night I was sitting with the auditor at around 3AM at the front desk when the elevator alarm went off. It was stuck and would not open. Well, it turned out the group inside was Madness. We managed to pry open the elevator door and out walked about 12 people!

Now I don't know off-hand how many people were in that group, but I know there were a few. Anyway, from that day on I called that group Crowded Elevator.

So that gives you some idea what it was like to work in Switzerland. They say if you work in Switzerland you learn a lot about hospitality and of course they are right. I learned a lot about everything but most of all I learned that when it comes to service there is never any room for excuses. Just like their trains that always run on time, so it went working there. Perfection was the requirement.

The Girl

My boss was a workaholic, so I always felt a bit overworked and under-appreciated. But what happened that really spawned bad blood between us was the case of the girl at the front desk. I really liked her but was unable to persuade to her to go out with me. My boss was a merciless teaser about it. Let me explain what occurred during those two years.

It began right from the time I started in early 1988. The Swiss are a very conservative people and I was a Canadian who was pretty boisterous and full of boundless energy. This was in due in a large part to the fact that I'd figured what I didn't know or felt a lack of confidence in I would make up in pure enthusiasm. Fake it till you make it, in other words. This meant providing an all-out effort at work and then getting up the next day and doing it all over again. Sometimes I would be working up to 10 days in a row depending on how busy we were. It probably felt like boot camp. But the feeling of being overworked was replaced by this crush I was getting on the girl at the front desk.

She was Swiss and her live-in boyfriend was from France. She was quite attractive to say the least and could speak four languages. She was very smart and she knew how to get the attention of someone like myself who was starting to work in a country where I knew no one.

Basically, I never felt like she left me alone. When I went out at night I would find her at the bar or if I went to the staff cafeteria she would eat right alongside me. It was almost like we were dating. Anyway, I found myself liking her more and more. Mr. S was even commenting on my interest in her.

Finally, I sensed that she was open to going out, so checking our schedules, I noticed that we had a day off together. A few days earlier I had brought up the idea to her and she seemed rather open to the idea. I wouldn't have thought of this idea if it was going to be a no. To be honest, the teasing was getting to be a bit much. It was time to go to step two!

The day had come to ask her, but all I got back was that she lived with someone else and couldn't go out with me. "How convenient," I thought! I said a few words to her to express my frustration, which didn't go over too well with her.

Not good because after that she avoided me. Didn't eat when I ate. Her days off were different from mine. The front desk was a few feet away from my desk and when we did work the same day no words were exchanged except if it was about work.

I was disappointed and upset about the outcome but at least I got the monkey off my chest, so to speak. The teasing and carrying on by her was over.

Now, Mr. S was an interested observer through all this. While all this was going on he encouraged me to make my move, so to speak, but when this happened he turned a bit ugly. He never let me forget and move on after this happened. I didn't know what it was about this guy. He would work 29 days a month and he had no life. I am not sure if he just didn't trust anyone when he wasn't at work or he had too much of a workload to take a day off. I know a lot of the work was passed on to me, so I don't think it was the latter.

After this episode I played things pretty close. I didn't talk to anyone about what happened but you could see that others noticed the sudden frostiness between her and I. I think that was why in the fall of that year she left her job and went to a hotel in Interlaken. I wished her well before she left. Our relationship finished on speaking terms. Cordial would be a good word.

My Dad had passed away in August after a short battle with cancer and she passed on her condolences to me. I had visited him in June for a week when I got the news he had 2-10 months to live. I was away in Munich when I returned with the message to phone home. The funeral was being held that day. It was not one of my stellar days downstairs in the cold refrigerator. I felt pretty lonely that day.

After she left for Interlaken, Mr. S would not shut up about her to me. "You should go visit her," he told me, and so on and so on. So there he was repeatedly instilling this false hope. Finally, I relented and went to visit her. The first time I went she was off so I left a note. About a month later I went back and said hello and she gave me a tour of the hotel. It seemed all right. I thought maybe we were making some progress. That was about it, though, and there were a few times we met while downtown but she was with her boyfriend. In fact, one time the four of us had a beverage together in the casino. Very awkward, to say the least, for me.

What I didn't know at the time was she was obviously in touch with Mr. S while all this was going on. Now I worked in Switzerland for two years and this went on well into the second year. Even when I was with another girl he would always remind me of this girl. It was driving me crazy.

Then one day I had enough. I wrote a letter in French so she would understand it and went to the hotel and gave it to her. This was with about four months left in my second and final year. I told her to phone Mr. S up and tell him to stop talking about us like it is going to happen and not to mention your name again.

That next day and for the rest of the contract Mr. S was totally upset! With that, he made me work even harder and his attitude was frosty at the best of times.

Then the topper came one night I was out with others having an ice cream at the Montreux Palace and I see four people walking together. They were Mr. S and her with the housekeeper and someone else. I couldn't believe it. The guy had his eyes out for her all the time.

Now it was my turn, I thought, to let him have it. From that moment on, I chided him non-stop about him and her. "How's it going? She would be good for you! So when are you two going to get hitched?" The roles were reversed now and even though he probably got further than I did, he didn't like his own medicine. He was too much!

Even when it was time to say goodbye the housekeeper, who was a good friend of hers, said upon wishing me well that it was too bad what happened between her and I. I think in the end she liked me a lot. I really believe that.

But you know the best thing to say is what I always said from then on. "It's just as well." If something didn't turn out as planned it was just as well. It kept me well in future experiences in the upcoming few years.

Things I Did and Places I Visited While in Switzerland

Working in Switzerland for two years gave me the opportunity that many people given the same chance would love to experience. Situated right in the heart of Europe, every day off I had I was going somewhere. When I had time, I took advantage of the great train service.

In Austria, I went to the city of Salzburg and stayed in a bed and breakfast on the same street on which Mozart was born. In Innsbruck, I went white water rafting on the Inn River. Austria I loved because it is one of those countries that is modern, yet has kept its culture and traditions that date back many years. The cafés where you get your strudel had bench seats and are always crowded. If there wasn't an available seat, someone would invite you to join their group. I enjoy classical music and the home of Mozart made me imagine what it would have been like to live back in the 1700s. Austria would be one place I would like to return to for a visit in the future especially to see Vienna.

France was another country that was very close to where I worked. On more than one occasion I took the TGV, the bullet train that sped along the tracks between Lausanne and Paris. This train would go so fast that in order to see something out the window you had to look back rather than forward. Paris was great. My Mother came for two weeks the second year and we were in Paris in 1989 when the 200th anniversary of the storming of the Bastille took place, that event that led to the French revolution. That was quite the Fétè to witness!

I also went to Chamonix where the first Winter Olympics were held in 1924. This was pretty cool. I took the gondola up Mont Blanc, one of the highest peaks in the Alps. It was 15 Celsius on the ground but on top where we got off the gondola it was -1 Celsius. The highest summit is called the Aiguille du Midi and when you are there another cable car is waiting for you to take you to Italy over the mountain. Are you kidding me! Go from one country to the next via cable car.

When I got on the cable car on the ground I was wondering how this could get us up to the top. The car held about 50 people and the ascent was stunning. Instantly you were real high up in the air. It was quite the rush you could say.

With a co-worker we went to Annecy in France, which was pretty beautiful as well. We did some paddle-boating on the lake that warm, sunny day.

I was lucky to find a spot to live during my first year in a town just outside of Montreux called Territet. A cook who was working at the hotel ended up finding work in China and he was in a house living in a furnished room with a private entrance. He asked me if I wanted it when he left. Of course! It gave me a chance to get out of the hotel, so I grabbed it. It was on the edge of a mountain and when I opened the curtains directly across I could see Evian France on the other side of Lake Geneva. What a view I had.

The family who owned the house kept the place empty for me till I returned for my second year. When I came back, it was like coming home. The room was immaculate. A separate entrance with my own key and with very little I had to pay for rent. This was a great spot to crash.

Visiting Italy, I spent a few days on the Amalfi Coast basking in the hot sun and drinking Peroni Beer. Italy has this baking hot sun so lying on a beach or lounging by the pool is a good idea. Italians are never in a hurry so when you are there you just have to slow down a bit. The train ride is great. I went to Milan as well. Once again you have to be impressed by the history of this country. I took the train ride from Brig to Domodossola a few times. The train was like a subway. About 12 miles of it went under a mountain. That was pretty wild!

Then there was Germany. I visited Munich a couple of times on the train departing from Zurich. On one of those trips I continued on to Garmisch Partenkirchen, the home of the 1936 Winter Olympic Games. A beautiful spot located in Bavaria where some of the highest mountains in Germany are found.

Of course, I covered just about all of Switzerland while I was there. One of the most memorable trips was the Glacier Express from Zermatt to St. Moritz where another Winter Olympic Games was held in 1928 and later in 1948. This train ride was pretty amazing. It went through mountains and some climbs required some chain links underneath to help grab and pull the train over the steep climb. The small towns along the way were fascinating and even the fourth language in Switzerland called Romansch was prevalent on the signs.

Another trip was to Gruyere where they make the cheese and you had to try a fondue after that visit. Interlaken and Gstaad were some other great places to visit along with the major city centers such as Lucerne, Lausanne and Geneva. Another pretty spot was Davos. I could go on and on, but you get the point.

Everyday was a holiday. Even close by you had Chateau Chillon, which was a place where Byron was locked up for a while. The rows of vineyards of Switzerland alongside the lake were picturesque.

How I Took a Bartending Course and Traveled for Seventeen Years

So my two-year stay was a memorable time. I learned how to do things properly, and despite the love triangle, I saw and did a lot. When I returned for the second year, I had to be out of the country for three months before returning. That would have been in March of 1989. But the owners wanted me back in February. I had to therefore enter the country at a point where I wouldn't get my passport stamped. They told me to enter into Switzerland from France where I mentioned Evian was earlier.

I flew into Amsterdam for my usual stay there and then I took a train from there to Paris. From there, I took an overnight train to Evian. Pretty nervous, I couldn't sleep a wink that night and arrived in the early morning. The boats were not running across the lake at this early hour, so I had to take a taxi.

I had 400 French Francs with me and I told the taxi driver I wanted to go to Montreux Switzerland. He said no problem but I explained that I was instead going to say to the border control that I was going to go skiing and on vacation. In other words, I did not want them to think I was heading to work. If they looked for the work permit they would have noticed I was not to start until March 15th. Then maybe they would send me back.

I got to the border crossing and I was chatting with the guy and he took my passport and looked at the picture and gave it back to me all smiling and wishing me a nice vacation. Four hundred francs for the taxi ride from France to Switzerland! I got there and the landlord was out.

Finally, the landlord returned home about noon and afterwards I slept for 18 hours. I was exhausted.

Later on in March I had to exit the country again. I chose Paris as the overnight destination and took the train a grande vitesse (TGV), returning the next day to Geneva to get the passport stamped. Then I took the chest x-ray once again like the previous year.

Yes, Switzerland was a great time and it changed my life. Traveling was for me, and I loved Europe. I was right into the history of the continent. While in Switzerland being so close to the Berlin Wall coming down was extraordinary for me.

Where To Now?

When I had about 3 months left on my second contract with the Hotel Eden au Lac in Montreux I started to think about what I was going to do afterwards. There was a hotel trade newspaper that advertised plenty of jobs in various hotels around the area in which I worked. Many of them were the ski resorts for which Switzerland is famous.

However it was a lot easier to apply for those jobs from outside of Switzerland than it was to apply from within the country. The reason was, being a foreign worker and on a 9-month work contract, I had to leave the country for three months before re-entering to work anywhere else in the country. Because of that, it would be hard for an employer to hold a spot for anyone who had to be absent for that length of time regardless of their qualifications.

So I started to look for opportunities elsewhere where I could capitalize on the education I obtained working in Switzerland. Once again, I started to think of going back to Montreal to settle, but this time with some clout. Not only would I have a great resume this time around, but also I knew how to converse in the French language, which before I was lacking.

I did, however, end up going to one interview for a luxury cruise ship that was going to be launched in a couple of months' time. It was the first ship of a few that was going to be built in Marina di Carrara in Italy. The cruise line company was Renaissance Cruises.

It was pretty funny, as I almost didn't go to the interview. The office was situated in Rapperswil, which was way on the other side of Switzerland just outside of Zurich. I looked at the train schedule and I had to take four different trains and the trip was going to take four to five hours. Working a lot and having only one day off I just wanted to sit back and enjoy the day rather than spend it traveling just for an interview.

After some deliberation I decided I should make an effort, as the ad intrigued me. After the experience on the SS Norway only a few years before, I was not in a hurry to go back and try working on a ship again. This one sounded promising, though, and with only 114 passengers on board, it didn't sound like I was going to be worked to death either.

How I Took a Bartending Course and Traveled for Seventeen Years

The interview went great. Paul was the guy who interviewed me and we hit it off right away. He wanted to hire me for November. I said I had to fulfill my contract, which would end in December. That was the way it was left and a couple of weeks later I got a letter saying that unfortunately I didn't secure a position with the company.

Quickly moving on, I had this thought that perhaps I could pick any place in the world right now to work. With just a few months cruise ship experience back in 1986 I had secured a job in Boston. So I decided from Switzerland I was going to send my resume to a bunch of hotels in Hawaii. I was there once when I was 16 years of age with family. But what about working there! What more could one want with beautiful weather, beautiful women, and beaches everywhere.

On the resumes I sent out, though, I made one mistake. I said that I would be in Hawaii about mid-January and that I would call ahead of time to set up a suitable time for an interview. It was a pretty presumptuous approach, but I thought it could work. All I needed was to call and make a connection. Fly twelve hours and six time zones away from Montreal and ace the interview. Pretty simple, right?

I left Switzerland after two memorable years to head back to Montreal just before Christmas. Back to minus 20-degree temperatures and lots of snow. My mind was set on Hawaii. My resumes would be there shortly, so I was planning at the beginning of January to call the places up where I sent my resumes to see if I had any shot of landing employment.

In the meantime, I did another not so smart thing. I went to the Four Seasons Hotel in Montreal and fell in love with the hotel. The Four Seasons Hotel chain is Canadian-owned and all of their hotels are top-notch. Very elegant and service orientated. If you stay there one time and you like white chocolate they note it and the next time you stay you have white chocolate on your pillow. That's the sort of service it was known for.

So I filled out an application and it turned out the General Manager of the Hotel was Swiss. I got called for an interview and then had a second one shortly thereafter. The position I was being considered for was assistant room service manager. It was an entry-level manager position that would be a foot in the door to move upwards later on.

I knew I was about to get hired. My mother was all excited because she thought I was going to settle down finally.

I started phoning some of the spots I'd sent my resume in Hawaii. I spoke to a few people. It was coming to the day when it was either going to be the Four Seasons Hotel in Montreal or a shot in the dark chance of going to Hawaii.

Here is when I feel like I should have been an explorer 600 years ago. Always taking the chance or the harder route. It was a Wednesday when I was going to get a call from the Four Seasons. I knew they were going to hire me. From all indications it was a done deal. The night before, though, on the Tuesday I finally got someone interested in me coming to Hawaii. I wanted to know if providing a work permit for a Canadian would present a problem for them.

In other words, before consenting to an interview, I wanted to know if I was the right guy for the job, would being a Canadian prevent me from working in Hawaii. I didn't want to go there without them first telling me the work permit wouldn't be a problem. The guy I was talking to was going to check it out for me, and I was to give him a call the next day.

The next morning the Four Seasons called and offered me the job. After all these years, I finally land something promising in Montreal. But I need to hear what the decision was regarding the work visa from the guy in Hawaii first before accepting the job at the Four Seasons. I threw my eggs in one basket and told the Four Seasons that I planned on going elsewhere and thanked them for the chance. In hindsight, I should have just waited one day before giving them a decision. I thought, though, that Hawaii was looking good.

On the other hand, did I really want to return to Montreal after travelling around for a couple of years? Probably not. A lot had changed. As I mentioned before there are some things you cannot go back to, but it bugged me that I left that door open and put the Four Seasons through the interview process. It was additional stress I did not need to endure at the time.

My mother just shook her head and that night I called back the guy in Hawaii and it was a negative. I had to go to Hawaii first. If I had some cash in my pocket to spare I probably would have just flown there and taken the chance. He thought I was coming anyway and by my resume it sounded like that was the plan. But I was going for some small commitment first. I knew if that call was a yes I would have had the job. I knew that I was only going there with, "yes, we can do the visa," reply over the phone first. That didn't happen and my cash reserves were running low.

In the end, it was too risky to fly 5,000 miles just to find out. Swallowing my pride, I didn't call back the Four Seasons either. So I put myself in a tough spot as to what to do. Hang around and find a job, or do something else exciting. It was January and freezing in Montreal. I had just spent two years away on my own having a great time. Why would I want to come home?

An Uneasy Time

There were a lot of reasons why I didn't want to come home and work. A lot of it had to do with the situation that was going on at the time.

I had come to the final conclusion that settling back down in Montreal was not going to happen. Too much had changed since I left to Switzerland only two years earlier. When I left to go to Switzerland, my Mother had already moved to Ontario, then she chose to move back to Montreal a short time after that. She then was planning on giving it another go back to Ontario, so she, to say the least, was very unsettled. Not to blame her for what I was doing, but I have to admit if she was stable I might have stuck it out.

My stepfather and I didn't keep in touch nor did I have contact with any other relatives on his side of the family. My friends, with the exception of one, had all disappeared in large part because I had moved around the last few years. That, along with lack of employment available, and the language issue, had dispersed everyone to different parts of the country. This all happened a decade earlier when we left Montreal so why I thought each time I came back it was going to be like it was before I don't have an answer. Sometimes you hope for things as they once were. That is what I was doing.

My father had passed away a little over a year earlier in August of 1988, so there was a void there for sure, and my brother, well you could say our totally different lifestyles didn't contribute much to our relationship.

Also, my friends were mostly in Europe. I loved travelling around and when I sat down to think about what I wanted to do, it was a choice of wanting to get the hell out of Canada or have a great time in Europe. The answer was obvious.

Up to this point, I didn't regret anything I did, but there I was, 30 years old soon to be 31, and I hadn't made any money or settled anywhere. I basically lived out of a couple of suitcases. I was always going toward something, but was it because I wanted to leave behind the past so badly? Now, at 55, I have to say I was leaning toward the latter reason. If things were so great, I would have stayed in Montreal.

Steven Nicolle

I have learned over the years that if you do something, there is a reason behind it. It is almost always for a good reason. If you are not happy, then you have to do something about it. Just do something. Drop the water cooler talk and do something. If it doesn't work out, at least you learned something in the process.

The following year I was determined to make it happen. What exactly happened though was not what I had planned.

So after some thought I set my sights on getting back to Europe. I spent the last two years in Switzerland and worked with people all over the continent, so it just made sense that I would try to get back there where I was having so much fun. That, I felt, was where my future was waiting.

It was late January of 1990 when I found out that I could obtain a work visa for the United Kingdom. If any of your grandparents were born in the UK then you could apply for what they called a UK Grandparent Visa. My grandparents on my Mother's side were both born in England so I sent away for a Photostat copy of their birth certificates and began to patiently wait for their arrival so I could hurry over to the British Consulate and get the visa in my passport.

I waited and waited, until four weeks later it arrived. During this time I was sitting on my hands at my Mother's place because my savings were running dry and I needed some money to get my butt over there and start looking for work. Time was going against me.

Eventually, I got my visa and bought a one-way ticket to Heathrow Airport. While in Europe I picked up some Hotel and Caterer Magazines, which were based out of the UK that contained plenty of job opportunities. I believed I would have no trouble getting hired.

My plan was quite simple. I would arrive at Heathrow and get a room downtown and use that as my home base to start applying for work. Without much money, I had to find something quickly, but I didn't think that was going to be a problem. I figured a week would be all I needed to find that dream job I was looking for.

So with my two suitcases and a carry on bag in tow I headed to London, England. My first challenge occurred when I arrived and found out that the $600 Canadian funds that I brought with me translated into less than 300 British pounds. If any of you have ever been to London before the only thing that is cheap is the beer while everything else costs twice as much as back home.

When I got to the airport I went to the accommodation board where many places to stay were posted with a direct phone number. I began to call some places and finally picked one on Sussex Gardens by the Paddington Tube station.

It was early morning after the all-night flight, so I wanted to get to this accommodation as fast as possible so I could settle in and start looking through the job postings. I took a taxi and the price of the ride was about 50 pounds! "Okay, so I won't be taking too many taxis from now on," I thought. I arrived at the hotel and the price wasn't too bad. With the breakfast included in the room rate I didn't have to worry about finding food first thing in the morning before starting out on my job search.

Living in downtown London was exciting to say the least. The hustle and bustle of the city was amazing. I got to know the subway system quite well and when I had time between looking for jobs and making phone calls or faxing resumes I was seeing Buckingham Palace and spending time eating the pub grub and quaffing down a couple of lagers.

This was no vacation though, and the days I hated the most were the weekends when the Human Resource offices were closed. My money was dwindling. I wasn't finding work as quickly as I thought I would. Despite the number of jobs posted, there were as many job seekers, so the process of selection was quite slow.

It was only a couple of weeks before I started dipping into my credit card and living off that. Not a good thing to do when each pound you put on is the equivalent of $2.50 on your credit card.

This hotel was not exactly the finest of hotels either. I laugh about one incident that occurred now, but at the time it could have put a quick end to my job hunt. One night while I was sleeping I heard a knock on my door. I heard a key turn. This guy started to enter my room. Bleary-eyed I asked him what he thought he was doing. The guy backtracked and politely excused himself while saying he must have the wrong room. I went back to sleep after locking the door once more.

The next morning, I discovered this guy had somehow got the master key for all the rooms and went ahead and robbed four rooms of their valuables while the occupants were out. I guess I must have been tired because after having an intruder like that enter the room, I just went back to sleep again. I should have notified someone after it had happened, but, then again, was there anyone around anyway? I mean, for someone to randomly enter room after room without being noticed seemed improbable.

Using all the resources I could, I picked up the Herald Tribune newspaper that I usually just read to get some hockey scores from back home. I noticed a food and beverage manager position open at the Wena Hotel just outside of Gatwick Airport. The only way I could get there was to take the Gatwick express train from Victoria Station and then take the hotel airport shuttle to the hotel.

At the same time, I had an interview for restaurant manager at what was going to be a new hotel in Ashford, Kent, called the Ashford International Hotel. This hotel was being built to coincide with the Chunnel that was being built underneath the English Channel between England and France for high-speed trains.

Now, did I want to be a restaurant manager or a food and beverage manager? Being part of a new hotel should have leaned me toward the Ashford International. However, having been the assistant food and beverage manager in Switzerland, the next natural progression would be food and beverage manager. The other factor was the Wena Hotel provided accommodation, while the Ashford didn't. I thanked the interviewer at the Ashford, who was very nice indeed, and took the Wena position.

Soon, I was taking the Gatwick express and shuttle to the hotel. I had a room in the hotel and was ready to get to work and start making some money and improving my situation.

The General Manager had mentioned some problems. Some staff were pilfering food from the fridges and it was found in their accommodations. All the while he was telling me this he was holding up a package of smoked salmon he found just the other night.

I talked to the chef who was a nice chap, but definitely overworked. He said that the place was a mess and that if he made a food order, he had to get it okayed by the accountant first and if the accountant didn't think the item was necessary, he just crossed it off the list. In other words, the accountant thought he knew how to cook!

So in practice it was just about making do with what he had, and that was it. Even food requisitions from stores couldn't be done on a daily basis. The chef could only make requisitions three days a week and needed special permission to get in the fridges any other day. In other words, he didn't even have the keys to his own stuff! So who had the keys? The accountant had them!

The dining room manager from France had not had a day off in a couple of months. He was a mess! The food was not great either, so he ended up a lot of the time apologizing and buying people drinks most of the evening. The service was terrible.

Even the front desk couldn't smile if their life depended on it. The way they greeted guests was atrocious. Like, "Hey, welcome. What is your name?" without so much as a smile. I couldn't believe it.

The staff accommodations they had were like drab barracks with no windows. So it appeared they were unhappy for a reason.

I figured my first job was to get the accountant to stick his nose out of the business of the chef. The chef had to run his kitchen and not let the accountant do it for him. He had to purchase goods for the meal service and in a lot of cases the accountant would just say no, he couldn't.

I proposed to the General Manager that the accountant should not meddle so much in the on-going food and beverage operations. Maybe it was the fact that both he and the accountant were friends, but my request seemed to fall on deaf ears. In any case, I should have looked into this situation more closely before latching onto the job. Here I was in hotel of horror. But, on the other hand, here was my chance to step up and fix it.

We had a head of departments meeting coming up and I was ready to come up with some ideas. Just in case, though, I got in touch with the Ashford International Hotel, should my ideas get shot down. Ideas that I knew would work especially if they wanted to stop the theft that was apparently going on.

I asked the Ashford if they might reconsider me for the restaurant manager position. Unfortunately, it had been filled, but there was an opening for assistant conference and banqueting manager. I had to be interviewed once again, though. It was Wednesday when I scheduled the interview for two days later. I had to have a way out should the meeting have the wrong outcome.

We had a heads of department meeting at ten in the morning, but I could make it later that afternoon if it was okay for them, at about three o'clock. This way, if the meeting was positive at the Wena I could always phone and cancel the interview.

Some ideas I was going to propose at the meeting included changing to daily requisitions as opposed to tri-weekly, and having a key sign in and out sheet to see who was going in the fridges with the goal of stopping the stealing of food that was going on. It was a start, I thought. Then afterwards, begin to work on putting some creative ideas to work with the chef and maître d' on how to bring people to the hotel to eat and drink.

The maître d' from France wanted the weekend off as he needed to go home to Paris to see his wife. He hadn't seen her in a couple of months, the poor guy. He was elated when I said, "Just go, I will cover for you."

My schedule for Friday after the meeting was clear. After all I was the food and beverage manager, right? But Saturday and Sunday I was filling in for the maître d' and also I was closing duty manager on Saturday night and opening and closing duty manager on Sunday. Sunday was going to be a long day.

Well, the meeting Friday morning lasted a couple of hours and as expected I was shot down. The general manager and accountant ganged up and remained in unison. Any changes were not welcome, so in other words, I was really hired to fill a vacancy. They were content with continuing on the same way. "Okay, fine," I thought. It was time for me to go."

I told the general manager I would be away for a few hours, but I'd be back in the very late afternoon to early evening. I went to my room and got changed quickly so I could grab the next shuttle to Gatwick to grab the Airport Express to Victoria Station. The train to Ashford Kent was over an hour from Victoria.

I got there around three for the afternoon. I got the job. Mentioning I had nowhere to stay, they said Monday when I arrived I could stay at one of their sister hotels. The hotel chain was Queens Moat House and they had hotels all over the place. Pleased with myself, I headed back knowing that I would be soon out of the Wena Hotel. I would work the weekend and make my getaway Monday morning.

I had not received any pay for the week or so I was there. Looking at it as free room and board, the only money I spent was on the trains to and from the interview.

I was going to go crazy being stuck at the Wena Hotel, so I had to leave. What is the point of sticking it out and seeing if anything would change? I had my chance to exit and being out in the middle of nowhere, I could see it was going to be difficult to move later on. It was such a hard place to get to and from anyway. Without my own transportation I only had that shuttle to escape.

I worked the weekend. On Sunday night I had dinner with the front office manager in the empty dining room and I broke it to him that I was leaving the next day. He worked in Switzerland as well and he couldn't stand working there either. We had a big dinner, wine and liqueurs and I signed off on everything. The accountant was away as well as the general manager. The hotel was quiet.

At 11:00 after my shift as duty manager I asked the girl at the front to give me a wake up call at 6:30 the next morning. I went up the stairs and finished packing my bags. I set my alarm just in case.

I was awake at 6 and got up quickly to have a shower. I got the wake up call at 6:30. At 6:55 I headed downstairs with my three suitcases. One in each hand and the other slung over my shoulder. Walking through the lobby I said hello to the front desk girl and looking ahead through the doors I could see that shuttle.

There was no one else around when I went outside. One man was in the shuttle and then just as I was getting on the accountant appeared asking me what I was doing and whether I was helping someone with their bags.

"Yes," I replied, "I am helping myself on with my bags. Thanks for the memories!" I still remember the look on the accountant's face as the shuttle closed the door and drove away.

I took that train to Ashford Kent then took a taxi to the Inn I would be staying at until I could find a place of my own. I gave the hotel a call when I arrived and was told to report at nine the next morning. The Ashford International Hotel had not yet opened, but we were in the midst of training new people for the opening that was soon to occur.

So that concluded my only Food and Beverage Manager position I ever had. An experience I wanted to forget about as soon as that shuttle pulled away to the train station. That one week felt like one year. As I was hustled away in the shuttle I remembered the words of Martin Luther King. "Free at last! Free at last! Thank God Almighty, free at last!"

Ashford, Kent

For me working in the hotel industry was always about the life experience more than the work experience. I mean service is the same everywhere. You serve and make people happy. But living in a different spot was exciting. Work was just something to give me some money to see or do things. Jobs like the Wena Hotel didn't work out for me at times, but I was someone who was always planning my next move no matter where I was working. Stability was not my strength. Taking chances was, though, and many times I faced the consequences of impulsive decisions. I liked the unknown factor, but it was not an easy way of doing things.

I was always short on money. Airplanes, trains, buses, and subway fares were what it was all about. A bite and a pint and off I went to the next spot wondering what would happen next on the journey. So there I was checking into the sister hotel of the Ashford International Hotel I was going to be working in. They gave me a week to find somewhere to live.

With the Wena Hotel behind me, I headed to work my first day full of vim and vigour, ready to make a good impression.

Charles, the conference and banqueting manager, was a decent guy about the same age as I was and for those of you keeping score, I had just turned 31 a couple of months earlier. They had already hired some banquet waiters and so we went about the task of conducting some training meetings on proper service.

The popular food service I am speaking of and very popular in England is that which is called Russian Service. This is when the waiter arrives in the dining room with a platter of food and gently and neatly places the hot food on the plate in front of the guest. After he or she does that, the sauce is passed over the main entrée, and voila, the job is done. If there is a soup service, you pass the tureen of soup with a ladle and fill everyone's soup bowl, which are placed beforehand in front of the guest. After the guests have completed their dinner, the tablecloth would be crumbed down and dessert and coffee or tea served afterward.

So, unlike Switzerland and other fine dining establishments I had worked in back in Canada, where the service was of the plated variety, this

Russian service was new to me. I might have touched on this back at the Troika Restaurant a few years earlier in Montreal and did the French service where the food preparation was finished off at the table at the Boulevard Club in Toronto. But other than those two experiences, the platter service was a fresh learning experience.

We were busy right from the start with many meeting rooms booked up on a daily basis with some bigger functions during the weekends taking place.

Working was not a problem at the hotel, but outside of the hotel my living arrangements were less than ideal. After the week of living it up at a nice hotel I found an affordable rented room in a big house.

There is a big difference between furnished rooms in England and Canada. First of all, the rooms over there supply a bed, but no linen. So I had to borrow linen from the hotel where I was staying. I hung one of them over the window to block out the sun. It was a bare room, you could say. It was a weird apartment, though. It was damp all the time and the bathroom was located right beside the kitchen. You had to walk through the kitchen to go do your business and run a bath. The only thing was there was no shower and the bath water used to trickle out. Therefore, you would take a bath in ankle deep water because you didn't want to run the water all day.

It was about a 25-minute walk to work. Fortunately, I don't remember it raining that often so I didn't get drenched walking at 6 am to start my shift as duty manager when scheduled.

The people at the Ashford were really happy with me so they gave me the job I had originally been interviewed for as the restaurant manager. The manager they had hired was not getting the job done. The team of 26 women waiters were ruling all over him and the service was not up to snuff so they asked me if I wanted to do it. I said, "Sure, I can fix the problems."

The restaurant had 126 seats and, to be fair, it was not that busy at all. Perhaps because it was a quiet open without much advertisement. These 26 waiters, though, were quite adamant about getting their days that were owed to them. Each came with their number of days off that were owed to them. I also had a list of my own that was kept by the previous manager of who he owed a day off. Both the waiters' list and mine were pretty much the same.

So up I put a day-off request sheet on the board for the waiters to fill out. The business was slow, so I began to give people two to three shifts a week. They began to complain because they needed the money. "Okay," I said, "but I have to give you days off because they are owed to you." After a couple of weeks of making no money at all they forgot about days in lieu owed to them.

Here is what I learned about waiting on tables. A waiter in the weeds is much happier in the weeds and making money than a waiter standing around with nothing to do and making no money. In fact, the team got better because their sections got bigger and, with my help, they were able to cope better. I emphasized that everyone help one another and we became a better team because of it.

We had a grand opening and it was a smash hit. All the waiters were happy and so were the big honchos of the hotel and Queen Moat House. I was doing a good job, I figured. I spent a lot of time working with the staff and getting to know them and what motivated them. The days off they wanted, they got. It was a good situation.

I was not financially-well. Although I did take a quick three-day trip to Switzerland to visit my old haunt back in Montreux. Maybe I was just hoping to get a glance of the girl I worked with that I had a crush on. But, alas, she was nowhere to be found. I took a ferry to Calais France for a day, but that was about it. Ashford was a nice place, but not your resort spot. Just middle-class working people trying to eke out a living, was what it was. "How long before I get bored of this existence?" I thought.

Getting to Ireland was on my mind, as I had been writing frequently to this girl I worked with the second year in Switzerland. I would write and get a reply a day or two later. She said she had someone back in Ireland, but I wouldn't have minded making the trip up there to Killarney to find out. She was really nice.

As far as lasting any length of time, though, the writing was on the wall. It was May and entering my third month at the hotel. I was making 10,000 pounds a year. That equated to about $25,000 dollars in Canadian currency. With England's cost of living, it felt more like $12,000.

I decided to go in to work one day and sit down and discuss my situation and whether they would consider giving me a raise. At least I thought it was what I needed to give myself some incentive to stay. The answer was, "We are happy with you, but the next pay raise review is not until the next January," which was still six months away.

Looking back, I could have toughed it out. But when you are broke, it doesn't matter where you are. You cannot do anything. I liked what I was doing there, but outside of work I had no life. I just remember going to the pub and standing at the bar ordering a lager top or two but no more. That was about it. I discovered living in a different country may be interesting, but it is no vacation. I did as much as I could but I was going broke doing it. I had to make other plans.

Heck, I didn't even make it to Ireland. All I could think about was getting enough money to head back to Canada.

Back to the Drawing Board

Upon the disappointing news that no pay raise was forthcoming until the following year, I made up my mind that given how expensive things were in relation to the 10,000 British Pounds I was making, it would be better just to put my tail between my legs and fly back to Montreal to think about what I wanted to do.

I gave my notice at the Ashford International Hotel and bought a 99 pound one-way ticket on Virgin Airways to New Jersey with a connecting flight from LaGuardia in New York to Montreal.

This was early May of 1990. I stayed briefly in Montreal, then headed west to Vancouver to start looking for work. My plan was to head out West because that was where the economy was booming.

I would apply to all the major hotels downtown. There was a whole bunch of them to apply to and I was going to go in at the very least as an assistant restaurant manager. I believed it was an obvious entry-level position, considering my just-finished stint as a restaurant manager and assistant food and beverage manager previous to that in Switzerland.

To save money, I traveled by Greyhound bus. Now, for those of you who might be wondering how far a trip that is on the Trans-Canada Highway from Montreal here are the gory details.

The bus left the Montreal terminal at 9 PM. I arrived in Vancouver at 3 PM, 66 hours later! Some highlights of the bus ride included 8 people getting kicked off the bus to an awaiting police car in Wawa, Ontario for smoking in the washroom. Where is Wawa? Well, that is in the middle-of-nowhere northern Ontario.

Some kid was put on the bus in Montreal and in Manitoba nearly two days later the bus driver asked him where he was going, to which he replied he didn't know. In fact, what happened was someone bought him an open one-way ticket just to get rid of him. He had no idea what was going on.

In Sudbury, a guy sat down beside me and we started talking about where we were heading. I said I was heading west to work in hotels. He said he was going to Edmonton to work in the oil fields. "Oh, that would be exciting," I said.

"Yes," he answered back with a twinkle in his eye, "there are a lot of guys up there." Yes, he was a male prostitute. Some interesting people you find on the bus.

The length of the ride was uncomfortable to say the least, but seeing Canada this way was exhilarating. I didn't sleep for the first two nights, but the third night I couldn't stay awake. Just getting out of Ontario took 30 hours. Ontario is huge!

Arriving that afternoon, I grabbed a taxi to where I would be staying hopefully for only a short time until I landed on my feet with a job and then a place to live. It was a friend of my mother's who we had known for a long time.

As quickly as I could the next day I started to hit the Human Resource Departments in all the hotels. Once again, I thought I struck gold with the Four Season Hotel in Vancouver. They were looking for an assistant restaurant manager in their Seasons Café.

I had one interview then another interview. I kept bugging them to ask if they indeed were going to come to a decision shortly as I couldn't hold out much longer. The man said I needed another interview with the general manager. He would give me a call at the end of the week. I didn't hear from him at the end of the week.

Meanwhile, I wasn't having much luck finding anything else in other hotels. I was looking to break through into management and not looking to take a bartending or waiter position. A lot of places wanted a Canadian reference overlooking the fact I had done anything in Europe. Certificates I had from Switzerland meant nothing. They wanted to talk to someone in Canada, which made it difficult.

The friend of the family who was nice enough to let me crash for a while was understandably wondering when I was going to land something. I could understand her situation, as the apartment was not big.

Finally, I called this guy up at the Four Seasons. The process was taking too long and the main stumbling block was, since the hotel was full of union workers, they might have been looking for someone who worked with unions before. I didn't understand that very well. I just wanted them to make a decision one way or another.

The following week I called back to tell them of my situation. "If, by Friday, I do not hear back and get this interview done, then I have to move out." He said to call back Thursday. Now, by this time I was flat out of money. I called back Thursday and Friday, and never heard back.

So here is what I did. On the Friday night I took an overnight bus to Oliver, B.C., which is situated in the Okanagan Valley to get a job picking cherries. I decided that I would like to do something completely different for a while to regain my focus. I left my good pants and shirts back in Vancouver because I wouldn't be needing them to pick cherries.

It was a hot morning, I remember, in Oliver. The bus arrived at 6 AM and I headed to the agricultural worker center to find out that someone would be picking us up around 9 AM. I left my bag there and walked around this small town of a few hundred people. "Wow," I thought, "this place is pretty beautiful." There was a mountain range where the rattlesnakes hissed. It was a place where people would spend the summer in their big trailers. Everything was pretty laid back, it seemed, although, it was way too early in the morning to see any hustle and bustle if there was any.

I was looking for a place to grab some coffee and some breakfast. Then I saw this hot-looking girl put out a breakfast sign in front of this restaurant. Not one to pass up looking at an attractive woman, I sauntered into the restaurant. I started talking to her and mentioned that I was a waiter and here I was picking cherries for the time being. I asked with the busy season coming up would they be looking to hire someone. She said, "wait till about nine, then the owner will be in and you can talk to him." I waited past the time to be picked up by the cherry picker boss.

I talked with the manager. He said he could use someone part-time. I said, "Great!" So I had to get back on the bus to Vancouver and pick up the black pants and shirt I left behind. I went back to the agricultural office and picked up my bag where I left it before I went for my stroll.

Having to hang around until the return bus trip arrived to take me back in the afternoon I had to find a place I would be able to sleep. An inn was attached to the restaurant. Unfortunately, there was not a room available in the entire town, let alone the inn.

Graciously, the manager said "Okay, you can crash in my room." They wheeled a bed into his room. For the next two months, I would sleep in that bed. There was hardly any room so space was at a premium. I thanked him for the job and space and the innkeeper for the bed.

I jumped on that bus again overnight to Vancouver and returned the next day by the same bus. The ride was about 6 hours each way. Between buses from Montreal to Vancouver and Vancouver to Oliver I was going on 80 hours total.

The waiting on tables was minimal. It added up to about 22 hours a week. All I did for July and August was go to the outdoor pool and live on minimal amounts of food so I could pay the minimum amount due on my credit card.

The first week I was there that guy called from the Four Seasons. He got the number from the friend I was staying with who passed it on. He asked me to come for an interview that week. I mentioned it to the manager and he said, "Either you go for the interview or stay here. If you go, so does your job."

I asked the guy one last time, was I going to be hired? I just can't leave this job unless you can tell me if I am going to be hired or not. I figured if this is going to be another stupid interview and then wait and see, I was not going to leave Oliver. Especially if it meant having to ask the family friend to stay over at her place once more.

He said he couldn't promise anything, so I said, "Thanks, but no thanks." No more bus rides for the time being and waiting on the edge.

I know it was a big move from England to Vancouver, but the slow decision-making process was frustrating. I was really ticked at what had happened and what I had got myself into. Here I was a couple of years earlier riding on the crest of a wave and now I was a part-time waiter making hardly anything sharing a room and sleeping on a cot. Thirty-one years old and broke!

Recruiting the Unrecruitable

The truth was, I didn't want to pick cherries. Let's make that clear right now. I was fortunate to walk into a restaurant for some breakfast and land a job as a part time waiter. If not, this story would have taken on a different direction.

I was tired of getting myself into these sticky all win or nothing dramas with these jobs I was getting. I missed out on the Four Seasons in Montreal at the beginning of the year because I wanted to go to Hawaii. Neither came to fruition. Then it was off to England and the Wena Hotel and afterward the Ashford International Hotel. Time ran out for me at the Four Seasons in Vancouver and there I was in tiny Oliver sharing a room with my boss and making little money.

I remember Oliver was hot. You couldn't live without air conditioning and most afternoons I would spend time in the public pool cooling myself off. Osoyoos just down the road close to the US border lays claim to having the only banana plantation in Canada.

So you could say I had a lot of time to think and that with the heat made me go to a Canadian Armed Forces Recruiting Center. I read something that they were holding an open information session in the nearby town of Penticton just north of Oliver.

I thought maybe that would be a cool thing. Do my duty for 20 years and then retire with a pension. That would be when I was 51 years old.

So I went and they were actually looking for cooks in the Navy, of all places. I thought that would be something I could do. I always wanted to improve my cooking skills. After that meeting, I followed up with, of all things, a resume, like it was a job interview. They said, "Great! Here are some forms to fill out."

Filling out those forms was gruesome! I had to go back 10 years with all the jobs I had and places I lived.

While I was filling out the forms, the restaurant informed me that it was time to go as the season would be winding down shortly. It was time for me to start looking. The time was about mid-August.

I picked up an employment paper in the job centre and saw that there were many openings in Jasper, Alberta right in the heart of the Canadian Rockies.

I called one place and they said, "Sure, come on down and there will be a job waiting for you when you arrive." I said I would be bussing it there and did not have any accommodation. They said, "No problem, we have a place for you to stay in the staff building."

Parting ways, I thanked the owners for their giving me an opportunity to work with them. I then went to the recruiting center in Penticton. They said I could take the oath and sign the papers for the Navy in Kamloops at the end of September. The exact date I cannot remember, but I do know the plan was to leave Jasper just before that and head to Kamloops for the swearing in to the Navy. I would stay overnight and then head to Montreal to rest up a bit before the Navy experience would begin.

I was, in the meantime, trying to get into shape by running 100-yard sprints interwoven with push-ups and sit ups in the hot sun. I felt like I was in pretty good shape for a 31 year-old. The keywords here are: "for a 31 year-old."

Working in Jasper was quite the experience. I arrived at the hotel and was quickly assigned a room with this other guy. He asked me if I was the new guy and then added that the room was just fumigated because the other guy I replaced had scabies. Scabies is a mite that gets under your skin that causes severe itching and rash.

"Super!!" I thought, "Wow, now I am going to not sleep at night if I start itching somewhere. I am going to think this mite has got me. However, they did fumigate the place so I shouldn't worry, right?"

I was scheduled to start the next evening. What I did the first evening was take a tour of the place and get a sense of where things were in the kitchen. I had one of the waiters show me around. Ice cream was left out and melting, entrees were being sent back, the chef was having a meltdown. It didn't appear to be quite the place I would enjoy working.

After the tour, I went to the restaurant next door in a place called the Lobstick Lodge. I had a brief encounter with the restaurant manager who told me he was looking for a breakfast waiter and would I be able to start tomorrow. I said, "sure but do you have any accommodation?" Yes, they did.

Remember, getting a place of my own was out of the question because in a few weeks I was heading to the Navy.

I slept at the first place that hired me and then the next morning worked at the Lobstick. I liked it and after my morning shift headed over to the restaurant I never worked in and said I had found something else. I also mentioned that this operation looked a bit of a mess when I went on the walkabout the previous night. The manager actually concurred with me. Such was the state of affairs in the restaurant.

The breakfast was busy and interesting to say the least. There were two girls and myself and the breakfast supervisor. Together we would do the bus tours that would come in as soon as we opened the door at 7 AM and work our butts off getting them out and then the leisure guests would arrive. Breakfast went till 11 then we set up for dinner and usually we were out by noon. That was it.

Then the supervisor quit and there was just the three of us to manage the hordes of people each morning. I remember one particular morning one of the girls had asked for the day off. The other girl thought it was her day off. I arrived that morning and started to put the creamers on the table and jams when I noticed that I was the only one that was coming to work. The breakfast chef came out and said, "What are we going to do?"

I said, "Just make sure the dishwasher watches the buffet and I will do my best to serve the guests."

There were two bus-loads lined up at the door. Luckily, they were seniors. When I opened the doors and everyone was being sat I announced to them that I would be their only server today. If you want something off the menu, I will get to you, but we have a beautiful buffet here for you. I poured that coffee and made their teas as fast as I could. I got meals off the menu for them. The dishwasher watched the buffet.

Then at 7:50 they all had to pay. They were honest enough. They all lined up nicely and brought their bill to me. No one complained and applauded my effort although what do you expect the tip would have been? Not much for the work, let me tell you.

Every table in the dining room was covered with dirty dishes. I started to bring the big trays out to clear one at a time. Then around nine I got hit again! I probably did another 25 people after that. I set up everything and got out at 2 PM. I made just over a $100.

The final cover count I did for breakfast that day was 120 people. That morning probably more than anything locked my name in Richard's head. He was the food and beverage manager, but he was usually at the other hotel where his office was located. Not a complaint he heard. The front desk didn't even know I was the only waiter on that morning. Richard asked me why didn't I call him. I said the obvious answer: that I was too busy, to which he laughed.

I left the Lobstick mid-September and headed to Kamloops for my induction. I was going to fly from Montreal to Halifax and be bused from there to Cornwallis for Basic Training. I headed home by plane this time and waited for the day of reckoning I like to call it. I signed up for three years.

In the Navy

It was after Thanksgiving in October of 1990 and I was on a train from Montreal to Ottawa to catch the Canadian Forces jet that would take a bunch of us to Halifax, Nova Scotia. From there, a bus would take us to Cornwallis and Basic Training.

I figured I was in pretty good shape for basic training. I could run a mile easily under 10 minutes and I was in as good shape physically as I had ever been since I was a teen. I thought this was going to be a walk in the park. That is what I thought in my mind anyway.

On the day, I grabbed a train from Montreal to Ottawa. At the Ottawa airport we were disappointed to find out we were flying commercial instead of going in the big Hercules aircraft. My first glimpse at what it was going to be like occurred on the bus ride from Halifax airport to Cornwallis. We stopped for a minute and stepped outside. It was time to get on the bus again and this sergeant is screaming at us to hurry up. "Whoa," I thought, "take it easy."

We arrived in the barracks about midnight and were given a lecture that lasted for about an hour and sent off to bed. As we arrived late, we were allowed to sleep in till 7 AM. After that it would be 5 AM wake ups.

The next day we were assigned our cots and told that during the night two people every two hours would be scheduled to be awake and be on watch for misbehaviour or fire. So it would be a real sleep-breaker if you were scheduled at 3 AM because that meant you would be awake till wake up call at 5 AM. Lights had to be out at 10 PM.

As it turned out, the only thing I liked was lights out and church service on Sunday. I hated everything about basic training.

The platoon sergeants made life really difficult, of course, as their job was to break us and mold us. Easy to do to an 18 year-old, but to a 31 year-old it was much more difficult. I was dead meat. They bent me and tortured me.

My boots were never polished enough so they would whip them out the window. My bed never was made well enough so they would tear it up. My kit was never good enough so they would tear that apart and make me do it over again.

The sergeant would scream in my face and I would look back at him in the eye. You are never supposed to look back, but straight ahead. It is a hard habit to break, not looking at someone screaming at you.

Drill was a disaster. I cow-kicked so much that my left foot kept coming down on the side of my right ankle causing severe bruising and bleeding. My swimming was not good enough so I had to take swimming lessons. I was fatigued like crazy.

This girl I was writing to in Ireland on a daily basis and phone calls back home were my sole enjoyment.

Then I became a problem for them. Not intentionally at first, but later on perhaps. One day the warrant officer gave us all a talk and he mentioned something along the lines that if we wanted to discuss anything his door was open.

It was around that time that I noticed our 30-minute lunch break was becoming a lot shorter each day. Sometimes it seemed that we barely got our food and then we were being called back on parade 20-minutes later. I was getting peeved off with that.

It happened a few times, and then I said to everyone that I was going to the warrant officer to talk about this. I would not get ready to be on the road at 5:30 AM. Instead, I would go right into the platoon office to discuss the matter.

The wake-up call happened and I went to the office where the meanest SOB of them all screamed at me. He threatened to send me to jail for dis-obeying orders. I was freakin' scared! The warrant officer got on the phone and told me to get in line and that he would talk to me later. Ooops!

Later on, the warrant officer told me to just go along with everything. He promised that once the ten weeks of basic training was over, things would get much easier.

Most of the time they had me going to the torture sessions at noon for something I didn't do right. The first time I went they yelled at me and told me to do 25 good push-ups. They were calling me by every name in the book. While doing the push-ups, though, I glanced up and saw them all snickering and smiling. I thought, "Okay if this is your game, I will play it too."

Disobedience became my trademark. At noon when I would be scheduled for the torture session, I would arrive a few minutes late to find a private doing knee bends outside the door. Sometimes the guy would be crying. I would ask him if anyone had mentioned my name or my whereabouts. He would say no and I would say okay and head off for lunch.

I left my kit as it was. I couldn't iron for the life of me, so it couldn't get better than it was anyway. My boots were scoffed and marked, so I couldn't get them cleaner than they were the day before when they got tossed.

The fourth week came and it was time for the gas chamber test. Before that, everyone had to march properly and salute at the sergeant's command. Just before it was my turn, I heard one of the sergeants say something to the other, causing them both to laugh as I began my march. Halfway through the marching drill I started to crack up. I was laughing and he just yelled at me to get to the side calling me a big failure with expletive language.

Now, to add more intrigue to this story, while I was in Montreal a few weeks earlier, my buddy Donald had mentioned that a friend of his was going to be in basic training around the same time I was and that maybe I would run into him.

Upon my failure to advance after the marching test, I was demoted back to another platoon to start once again. Alone in the barracks, I was sewing my new platoon number into my different uniforms and clothes. It was during this time my new platoon members entered the room.

Lo and behold, who was the first guy to come over and say hello but the guy I heard of back in Montreal. He said, "I heard you would probably be here." I went on to explain what had happened and how my kit was not up to snuff each time it was inspected. He said he would help me with that, no problem at all.

"Great," I thought. Finally I could get a bit of help from someone else that might get me through this.

So what I did was become even more rebellious. We were told to get haircuts the next day. We are marched off to spend another $5 on a hair cut. One, I felt I didn't need to as I had just gotten one in the last platoon a week ago. "What a waste of time," I thought.

So there we are taking turns in the chair and it was breaking now into our lunch period. My stomach was grumbling. I said to the guy beside me, "I am making a run for it. I am not waiting around, I am hungry," and I took off.

That night in the barracks we were lined up for inspection. The sergeant was screaming at us from the back of my neck saying that if anyone did not get a haircut today they better tomorrow or there will be a price to pay. Now, I figure this guy is looking at the little hairs growing under my line at the back of my neck. A sure sign that I was the one who didn't get my hair cut that day.

I grabbed my friend after and told him I needed his help. I handed him my razor and asked if he could just evenly shave the nape of my neck where any small hairs might be so it would look like I indeed did get a haircut. He did and I never got a haircut. I knew they knew, but no one blinked.

It was obvious I was not cut out for this. In the field of combat, the guns would fire and I would probably be running for my life. Besides, everyone wanted to go to Iraq to be in the Gulf War that was going on at the time. That thought didn't excite me at all. Why did I enlist anyway? Meanwhile, my drill was not improving. My marching was laughable. However, I did manage to have more confidence in the deep end of the pool.

How I Took a Bartending Course and Traveled for Seventeen Years

I had been in basic training now for seven weeks but only three counted as I was put back. I knew I wasn't cut out for this at all. It was on a Thursday when we were told that the inspection on Friday morning would tell who was going to be inspected at noon on Saturday by the big chief. So we had better have our kit in order Friday morning. My buddy was the platoon leader and had a kit that was immaculate. He said he would give me a hand.

He did my entire kit. The Friday morning inspection took place and the guy came around and looked at mine. He trashed it. Afterwards, my buddy came over and said he was completely surprised that it was trashed. It was perfect. The ironing, the folding of the shirts right down to the rolling of the socks was done exactly the same as his kit. I thanked him for what he did. I guess they were on to who was helping me out. I was right, because that afternoon the commanding officer called him aside to tell him not to help anyone.

Now I was on the big guy's inspection at noon the following morning. I had enough. I tried my best to iron my clothes properly and do my kit as well as I could but when 10 PM and lights out had arrived, I said to myself, "This is it. Screw it!" I left the kit half-done and had my first good night's sleep in seven weeks.

Noon came and there were about five of us on. The big guy came to mine and just looked at it. He said, "Nicolle what are we going to do with you!!! What do you want to do!!"

I said right back, "I want a release."

He yelled back, "What!!"

I said, "A release, Sir!!"

He just looked at me and walked away. Later on that afternoon I had an appointment with the lieutenant major, the really big guy.

Sitting in the waiting room, I noticed the young guy who was being discharged come out crying. I thought, "This is going to be harsh." Instead, it was all cordial and he even mentioned that I appeared like I was actually improving. I said, "Yes the ironing and my kit was holding me back."

I signed my release papers and for a week I walked around in my civilian clothes handing back my kit.

At 4 AM on Saturday the week after, I was loaded on a bus to Halifax airport with about 20 others. All of us were being discharged for some reason or another.

Listen, I have a lot of respect for our people in uniform. They put their life on the line for us everyday, but for me this was a mistake. It wasn't for me.

I was out of there and on my way back, this time to Toronto. It was heading into December by this time and Christmas was around the corner.

What a year it was. Lots of mistakes, you can say. Experiences that one can laugh at now but then it wasn't that funny. It changed me somewhat. It made me stop and think about what I was doing instead of just going and doing it. Another thing that happened was after all the crap I took at basic training, my character was hardened. I wasn't about to take any crap from anyone after what I went through in basic training. The timing couldn't be worse.

A Bad Ending to a Bad Year

The disastrous time at basic training brought me to the beginning of December and I was back in Toronto. This time I was staying with my brother, his wife, and three nephews and niece. My mother was on the road, moving and living somewhere in a room. It is sometimes when things like this happen it is good to have your mom to go back to and regroup. In this case, I chose my brother. Not a good idea.

At the time, I figured it would be a good time to catch up with my brother and stay Christmas, then move on to the next job wherever that was going to be. Instead of it turning out that way, the tensions were high. I guess I got on my brother's nerves. Some of the long distance calling I was doing was about looking for jobs and a couple of others were phoning girls, especially that one in Ireland. I had every intention of paying for the long distance I was accumulating during the stay.

Then there was some misunderstanding and I was given the boot on Christmas Day. On Boxing Day I headed to my stepmother's and stayed with her and my two brothers from my dad's second marriage.

I think I was so pissed off at my experience with the Armed Forces and mad at myself at the same time that I vowed that I wasn't going to take any crap from anyone, after being yelled at for seven weeks in the Army. "Kick me out on Christmas Day and you will not see me again," I thought.

My brother and I didn't talk for six and a half years after that. Never saw him again till 1999. I paid my long distance bill and that was it. My mother, instead of trying to fix the situation, chose my side and she didn't talk to him for the same amount of time. Not good when you have parents choose sides.

I guess I felt obligated to spend time with some member of the family during the holiday season. Maybe getting the heave-ho that Christmas I came to the realization that it didn't matter anymore. Maybe I should make some serious decisions about my own life. Choose some path and get on with it. Early on it was always about settling in Montreal. But after heading to Switzerland and traveling and working in England, who needed a family at holiday time?

How I Took a Bartending Course and Traveled for Seventeen Years

While at my stepmother's place I did find a job with a restaurant chain that was going to open a restaurant just down the road. I had to travel to another restaurant out of town to get trained for it. Getting a lift from a co-worker, I went to a few training sessions, but packed it in. It is a small world, but that chain of restaurants I worked at years later.

Sleeping on a couch with a few hundred dollars in my pocket and the memory fresh in my mind of the fight with my brother, I just wanted to get as far away as I could.

I noticed this ad in the paper of this resort in Field, British Columbia that was looking for a restaurant manager. I set up an appointment with them to say that I would be coming and, taking into account the bus schedule, arranged the interview time with them. It was January of 1991 and here I was getting on a bus from Toronto to Calgary. Only 48 hours this time!

Packing my two suitcases, all I can remember about January of 1991 was it was freakin' cold. The bus ride, like the one I took only a year earlier that took 66 hours, was brutal, as usual.

Field is a small town located right on the border between Alberta and British Columbia. Nestled in the Rockies on the Trans-Canada Highway it was a beautiful spot covered in about five feet of snow! The temperature was hovering around -18 Celsius. I phoned the lodge from the restaurant along the highway and told them I was here for the interview and asked if someone would come and pick me up as it was quite a trek on a snow-covered road to get there.

I waited over an hour for someone to arrive. Not a good sign when you are heading to an interview. I got to the front desk and introduced myself and asked for the person I was supposed to speak with about the job.

He came and gave me an interview for about a half hour. At the end of it he said, "Okay, I still have a few more interviews to go through."

"Wait a minute," I said, "I just took a bus from Toronto to be here and to start immediately." I went over my experience again and what I could say that would convince him that I was the man for the job.

"No, I understand," he said, "but I want to conduct some more interviews."

"Okay, that is fine," I said, "but you have to help me out now."

He wondered what I meant when I said that.

"Well, I have no car. It is getting dark out and the buses don't pass by here this time of day. In other words, I was totally committed to landing this position. You have to put me up for the night."

I was put in staff quarters for the night, and, without saying goodbye, headed out the next day to Banff and their job office to see what I could scrounge up. I didn't know where I was going to end up that day.

While at the job office, I gave a call back to my stepmom and she told me that Richard was trying to get a hold of me. "Great," I thought, "my saviour, Richard remembered me and called to hire me back."

I called Richard right away and he said, "Come on back to Jasper." He needed me to wait on tables. Thanking him profusely, I then proceeded to take a bus to Lake Louise and hitch-hike my way up the rest of the Columbian Ice Field Parkway to Jasper.

The temperature was colder that day and the sorry sight of me hitchhiking at the side of the road with two duffle bags and a suitcase freezing my butt off got the sympathy very quickly of some Swiss tourists who gave me a lift to Jasper.

I arrived at the Amethyst Hotel and got a hold of Richard. He put me in staff accommodation till I found a place. I began to work breakfast and some evenings as well. Not yet a busy time in Jasper. I secured a room in a house for $275 a month. I took a cash advance on my credit card to pay the first month.

It was January 5th I got that room and started work ready to turn the page on a horrendous 1990. From Montreal to England, Vancouver to Oliver B.C., Jasper back to Montreal then on to Cornwallis, then back to Toronto and now Jasper, Alberta. Two countries and four provinces in one year! With that and the jobs and basic training, I just wanted to stay put somewhere.

What a mess I was, but Jasper was the best spot for me at that moment. I needed to find some focus.

Rocky Mountain High in Jasper 1991

So after leaving 1990 behind and setting myself up in Jasper, Alberta, I was ready to start making some money and get back on track.

I started where I left off the previous summer working at the Lobstick Lodge doing breakfast and working some evenings at the sister hotel a few blocks away. Richard was happy to have me back and, believe me, I was happy to be back, away from all that had happened to me the previous year.

One thing I have never minded during my waiter career is working breakfast. Either people hate it because they don't like getting up in the morning, or they love it. I always have been an early riser and getting up in the morning to work the breakfast shift meant I had to be there at 6:30 AM. The ten-minute walk to work each morning with the beautiful scenery of snow-covered mountains was, for me, exhilarating. Along the way, you would see a few elk or deer eating some leaves off the tree in someone's backyard. It was very fun to watch.

It was different working this time in the mountains. Unlike the isolation I felt at the Saskatchewan River Crossing back in the summer of 1983, there was a lot more to do in Jasper.

The people you worked with were there for the same reasons. There was hiking, fishing, mountain biking, or whatever else you wanted to do. I bought myself a mountain bike and rode all over the place. Up and down hills and through trails. I was having a blast.

I would work till about noon at the breakfast job, and then take a few hours off before heading to the other restaurant to work dinner. On a day off, I would head to my favourite restaurant and have a king-size breakfast and read the newspaper for an hour. My days off fluctuated between jobs. Some days I would have the morning off and on another day I would have the evening off. Pretty much I worked at least one job every day.

Unlike a lot of the seasonal workers there, I would bank as much as I could. After my evening shift I would head to the ATM machine to deposit and leave myself some beer money for the nightclub. I hardly ever remember being in my room at all unless it was to sleep. There was a phone available to us if we needed it, but I never once remember using it. Sometimes

I would still be writing to that girl in Ireland. That came to an end midway through the year, though, when I asked her to come to Canada for a visit. She said no for all the reasons I knew already. I wrote her a goodbye note soon after. It was time to move on. Leave the past behind, so to speak. I was turning over a new leaf.

There were plenty of jobs. You could literally leave a restaurant next door and find another one a block away. As the summer approached I started another evening job at this Greek restaurant called the Palisades Restaurant. It was family-owned and I was the main man there. So main-man, in fact, that I was required to start at 4 PM to vacuum the entire restaurant. The owner would only pay from 4:30 though when the doors opened.

One of the things I remember most was that dessert trolley they had. I would have people salivating for dessert when I wheeled that around to their table. The owners loved it. The place was hopping all the time.

Jasper had a population of 3,000 people but each night 25,000 visitors would be sleeping in their accommodations and they all had to eat. There was a restaurant every other door to feed the masses. Tour busses, hikers, families on vacation, and the people who worked there all had to eat. Honestly, if anyone had kitchen utilities to cook they probably never used them. Why would anyone want to stay inside?

Throughout the year I was stashing the cash away.

A friend there suggested I work at his restaurant through the lunch hour. This was the same time I was doing breakfast and dinner. I only did it a few times before I realized that it was a bit much. I would make it there no problem for lunch, but it wasn't a high turnover restaurant, so you would get these campers still sitting there at 3:30. Getting from there to my evening job a half hour later was tight and I was getting stupid with work. That was what it was like, though, a Mecca for employment.

I remember I took a few days off when my friend whom I worked with in Switzerland came for a visit. We rented a car and went to the sunny Okanagan Valley in British Columbia.

Another time, I remember going on a hot summer day to this river that was fast-flowing from the melting snow on the peaks of the mountains. Stripping down and getting my whole body into the freezing water was memorable. Took only about ten minutes to dry off and warm up afterwards, though.

During the fall mating season the elk out-numbered the people in Jasper. Once summer was over the people left. It was shoulder season, which occurs after the summer rush and before the winter ski season. I would walk home after my evening shift and all over the place were these big elk. Being near a big elk is not a fun thing during this time, as they can become pretty protective. The big elks ruled!

As the summer season ended the seasonal staff left to go back to school and only the year-long inhabitants remained. Restaurants closed for the winter as many of them worked everyday for seven months and now it was time for vacation. It wasn't worth it for the independent restaurants to stay open for the winter, as the ski season in Jasper was not half as busy as the summer season.

The Icefields Parkway would close soon due to the amount of snow. Now to get to Jasper you had to go north to Edmonton, then head south again. The trip would take about four hours. Unlike Banff, which was a short two-hour trip from Calgary in the south.

When I taught the bartending course, I always talked of my time in Jasper. I always recommend to a young person, especially one in the food and beverage industry, to go work there for a summer just for the experience.

For me, it was an oasis of tranquility after the previous year. I was honing my craft as a waiter after giving management a shot the previous couple of years. The pubs and bars and outdoor life were addictive. The lifestyle was easy. Literally, there was no stress living there at all.

I did some white water rafting, hiking, bicycling, and met lots of people. I was in great shape. Jasper was one of those great experiences I would never forget.

A Missed Opportunity Leads to An Unexpected Phone Call

Halfway through the year while I was having a good time in Jasper, I was speaking to a couple of waiters who spent their winters working in the Cayman Islands. I thought that would be very cool and wanted in on it, so I asked them how I would go about doing such a thing.

One guy who had been doing it for a few years in a row explained that beginning in the fall season, employers on the Grand Cayman Island would begin hiring for the busy winter season that was about to take place. All I had to do was send down some resumes and follow up a couple of weeks later. Once I was hired, I would be down there around the end of November, which was perfect because that was when the slow season would begin in Jasper.

This particular guy who had been down there a few times told me of a few restaurants I should apply to and that once I got a job and flew down I could stay with him until I found my own place. Thinking back, it sounded pretty dodgy, but I was so used to jumping into the unknown that flying to the Cayman Islands to start a job was not a big deal compared to 1990 when I flew to England with only 500 British Pounds without a job waiting for me. I had learned from that experience.

I sent my resumes out and followed up with phone calls until one restaurant owner asked if I would be available for December 1st. I said sure and he mentioned that I would have to pay my way there. I wasn't thrilled about that, as flying to the Cayman would mean I would have to buy a round trip ticket which was kind of pricey.

But the fact the Cayman dollar was worth one and a half times that of the American dollar and at that time our Canadian dollar was hovering around 80 cents American, well, it was obvious to me I would make my money back quickly. The Cayman Islands were far from a cheap destination.

It was mid-November and I got my police check and my test for HIV completed. I was waiting for my employer to call and tell me to go ahead and book my ticket. He had to work on the visa, so I could work there. It was a juggling act because at the same time this buddy of mine had already left for the Caymans to go back to his job and I wanted to give him a date and time when I would be arriving.

The last week of November arrived and still I hadn't heard from this guy yet. If I was to be there the following week, I had to know whether it was a go or not. At this time, I was not working either because the restaurant I was working for was closed for the winter.

Finally, at the last minute, I got the word that I didn't have the job at all. The recession had begun and the outlook for the winter tourists did not look good. Hence, I was out of luck.

The recession of 1992 was in its early stages, and, unfortunately, when a recession hits all these sunny resorts that rely on the vacationer they suffer a severe drop in business. It is their meal ticket and if bookings are low everything suffers.

As I recall, that was a pretty big recession. When I travelled through Jasper a couple of years later during the summer that job board filled with restaurant jobs back in 1991 was empty. The hospitality industry really tightened up during this period.

So what was I to do? Jasper was great, but there wasn't much going on in the winter there. So I decided to try a select few cruise ship companies. I went after the small to mid-size cruise ship rather than the gargantuan SS Norway type that I was on five years earlier.

I sent about six resumes out and waited to see what would happen.

About ten days later I received a telephone call. After saying his name was Paul, the man asked if I remembered him. I replied, "No, not off-hand. I don't," and then he said he interviewed me in 1989 in Rapperswil just outside of Zurich. The only interview I ever went to while in Switzerland! I was delighted, and as soon as he mentioned the interview I knew who he was.

He told me that Renaissance Cruises was now getting ready to set to sea their seventh ship and asked if I would like to come aboard as a waiter. I didn't say yes right away. I asked him what the living conditions were like: Was it clean? How was the crew food? How long was the contract? I asked these and other important details that I didn't ask the first time around back in 1986.

It was all positive, and then the big question I had for him was how in the world would I get there. The ship was being built in Marina di Carrara in Italy. Paul said that was not a problem. He asked which international airport was closest to me and I replied, "Edmonton."

"Okay, we will DHL a ticket to you and you will get it in 3 days."

"Wow," I thought, "here I go to Italy."

A few days later I got the ticket and I was flying out on January 5th. Exactly a year to the day that I arrived in Jasper. Now it was 1992 and I could tell already it was going to be a hell of a year!

I guess it was worth making the trek to Rapperswil that day. The interview for a job I didn't get back in 1989 turned out not to be a waste of time after all. In fact, you could say it started a life-changing event for me.

Renaissance Cruises

It is January 4th, 1992 and the start of my new adventure. That is, working with Renaissance Cruises and taking part in the opening of their seventh ship that was to be named Regina Renaissance.

My flight details had arrived by DHL Express a week earlier. I would fly out of Edmonton to Toronto, then on to London, England. Then I would catch a connecting flight to Pisa, Italy where I would be picked up and taken to the shipyard where the ship was being built in Marina di Carrara.

I spent the night before in a hotel that had a mall attached to it. The only reason I mention this is on my day of departure I was up early and walking around the mall. It was just before the stores were about to open. I was on the third floor leaning on the railing overlooking the atrium admiring the décor when suddenly on the opposite side from me, a man jumped. The next thing I knew the paramedics arrived trying to revive him. Before my eyes that morning, I witnessed a suicide.

"What a stark contrast," I thought. Here I was embarking on an exciting experience and there was someone else in the deepest despair, taking his life. It shook me up a bit.

I remember the flight to London had to be rerouted to Glasgow, Scotland because pretty much all of England was covered in thick fog. I arrived a day late to the ship.

For a waiter, an opening of a ship is not a big deal. Most of the time we spent just lounging around and going out for an espresso in town. The only time we were really needed was to take the garbage lying around to the dumpster.

The fun thing was once the ship was ready it would do it's sea trials en route to Monte Carlo where we would spend 10 days taking on supplies for the ship. We all looked forward to that and even if it was January it started to warm up nicely, feeling like spring in this part of the Mediterranean.

The crew was great and the dining room team was mostly from Europe. While in Monte Carlo, we had a couple of dinners to serve to invited guests. Working as a waiter on a ship took a little getting used to just because of the flow of the entire dining experience. Everything was fast. For example, if you ordered five salads they were ready to pick up. You just went to the salad station and called out, 'three green salads and two Caesar salads,' and away you sped off to the dining room with tray over your shoulder. Service was pretty quick.

Soups you ladled out yourself. Very easy since the bowls would be set up beside the soup where you would pour and bring them out on a big tray. All your under liner plates and doilies would be at your station set up as part of your preparation beforehand for dinner service.

You worked as a team. There was a front waiter and a back waiter. The front waiter would take the order and the back waiter would run and get the food. The back waiter had to watch the line and time just about when the salads would be finished and fire the entrées to the kitchen. The front guy would hurry to clear the plates and make sure all the extra cutlery was removed from the table.

The back waiter would run out the hot plates with their cloches on top and you, the front waiter, would lift them off and deliver the right plate to the guest. It all went by seat number, of course, so if you were busy at another table, the back waiter would put them down for you.

Communication between the front and back waiter was important. Sometimes over the time I spent on the ships I would be paired up with a personality that didn't work well with my own and we had to be split up. This was not uncommon.

I was both back waiter and front waiter on the ships. The back waiter, as I mentioned, was responsible for running the food out and making the coffees and firing the soufflés on the farewell dinners. The front waiter took the order, put the food down, offered bread and water throughout the meal and cleared the plates nicely and put them on the tray. Not hard, but if anything went wrong it was the front waiter's fault.

In Monte Carlo the loading went quickly. Going out to the clubs at night, there was one time I drank for free. Getting low on money, I went to this club one night and they said if anyone would like to do karaoke they would get a free beer. I thought that was a pretty good deal, so I sang "Suspicious Minds" five times that night before they said they wouldn't allow me to do it anymore. Too bad or I would have just kept singing. I guess I was either drinking too many free beers or my voice was fading away.

As usual, the dining room is always the last department on board that is ready to go. Opening up a ship, everything, such as tables, chairs, cutlery, plates, glasses, remain covered until the last minute because unwrapping them early would only mean they would be covered in dust and you would have to clean them again.

Fortunately, in this case, the ship would be travelling empty till we hit Suez, Egypt where the passengers would embark.

I have to tell you, passing through the Suez Canal for the first time was really neat. Along the way you could see an old army tank not in use since the war between Israel and Egypt in 1967. Someone just abandoned it when the Seven Day War ended that year.

It was quite an ordeal getting alongside the pier in Suez. We were anchored in the bay for a few hours until the port authorities secured us a spot. Apparently the bribe was more cartons of cigarettes to the port agents.

Our first Red Sea cruise was to take place the following day, on February 8th. Arriving and finally getting off the ship on the 7th, we headed for Cairo and nearby Giza to see the pyramids. It was a great way to spend my 33rd birthday!

On the 10-day Red Sea Cruise we visited ports like Safaga and Sharm el Sheik in Egypt and Aqaba in Jordan. In Safaga the passengers would head to Luxor for an overnight stay so the ship was empty for an entire night. It was always party time. A big BBQ on deck with alcohol flowing. The first big party, we had a Norwegian bartender jump from the top deck into the water. The chief officer went nuts on him and sent him home. It wasn't a bright idea to jump off a ship.

Hurghada was not far away, so we all hit the disco every free night in Safaga. Aqaba in Jordan allowed us the chance to see Petra the lost city, which was featured in the Indiana Jones movie. After a couple of months in the Red Sea we headed back to the Mediterranean.

Meanwhile, they needed some crew for the next ship to take to the high seas. Renaissance 8 was being built and I volunteered to go on that ship. So midway through my six-month contract I headed back to Marina di Carrara to open up the eighth ship.

I didn't like the crew as much on the eighth ship as I did on the seventh ship, but I really got a chance to see more places. To go through the list of countries it would go like this from beginning to end:

Egypt, Israel, Jordan, Cyprus, Turkey, Greece, Italy, Spain, Portugal, France, Principality of Monaco, Belgium, Netherlands, Germany, Denmark, Sweden, Finland, Estonia, and Russia.

The question most people always ask is did I get the chance to see much of the sites at each port. I have to answer yes. Because we only had 114 passengers, and many of them were aboard for the shore excursions, we were free most of the time during lunch to see the sights.

It was the beginning of August when I disembarked in Stockholm to visit with this girl I met on the first ship. I got a surprise postcard from her when I left and kept in touch. She lived just outside of Goteborg in a small town. That was a lot of fun and for the next couple of years she would remain pretty close.

It was a great decision to join Renaissance Cruises as you will note in the upcoming chapters, but there was still one thing I wanted to try. So I did only one contract before I decided to embark on another road. It was a crazy set of circumstances that was to take place.

Summer of '92

It was during my contract with Renaissance Cruises that as a waiter I thought I had reached my full potential and I had accomplished what I set out to do. That was to travel, and I figured I had seen all I needed to see.

I was saving a whack of money on the ship so I decided that this time I was going to take a course and move into the kitchen. It seemed like an idea revisited, but this time I wanted to open up a bakery. You know, specialize in cakes, croissants, and chocolate.

The famous Cordon Bleu School out of Paris had just opened a couple of years before a satellite school in Ottawa. I enrolled in their basic pastry course beginning the month of September through December. The course went twice a week and upon graduation you could go on to the advanced course, which unfortunately was not available in Ottawa. You had to go to Europe for that.

There were just a couple of challenges I faced upon moving to Ottawa. I wanted to live cheaply somewhere and not sign any lease agreements. After the course ended, who knew what opportunities lied ahead and I wasn't yet sure that I wanted to go to Europe and complete the advanced course either. I wanted to keep my options open.

When I arrived in Ottawa, I picked a bed and breakfast to stay for a couple of weeks. It was pricey and I was soon going to run out of money if I continued to stay in it. The course was expensive as well so the initial expense was a hit in the wallet.

While staying at this B&B, I met this Scottish couple that had just immigrated to Canada and they mentioned that the YMCA had living quarters for temporary residents who were in transition. I thought, why not check it out? So I did.

I ended up getting a nice room with the showers and washrooms situated down the hall. It was really clean and I was really impressed. With living arrangements settled, I just needed to find a part-time job or two with some flexible hours.

With my ever-increasing work experience, it was not too hard to find. The first job I got was at the Chateau Laurier right beside the Parliament

Buildings in Ottawa. For those of you who do not know, Ottawa is the capital of Canada, so all the time you would see politicians holding news conferences or private dinner right in the hotel. It was a pretty exciting place to work. My shifts were varied as I worked in the banquet department as a bartender or waiter. Most of the time I worked as a waiter and had the delight of serving such personalities as King Gustav of Sweden and the oldest survivor of the Titanic at the time.

I also found work at the Ottawa Congress Centre. That was a huge venue where the biggest parties in Ottawa took place. I remember one in particular was a Christmas party for 2400 people. I was starting at one o'clock that day. The forklift would bring the tables in and there were four people working just to put the tables up and position them in the right place. Then a few others would start slapping the table cloths down and a few more started putting the cutlery needed for the 12 tops on the table. A few others would put the side plates down etc., etc..

It was fun to watch. It was like time-lapse photography when you see a building go up in fast motion over a long period of time. By 6:30 the candles were lit and the people sitting down to dinner.

We worked in teams of two serving five tables or 60 people.

The first course was already on the table, which was easy enough as the guests helped themselves to a couple of platters of antipasto. Then we served the soup from a tureen ladling the soup out into the bowl in front of them. Not so easy to do as the tables were tight. Then the salad and finally the main course, which we had to place on the plate on the table from the platter we held on our arm. The service was fast and furious and once the dessert and coffees were done, we were all in the staff dining room getting our own bite to eat. It all took about 90 minutes.

I did a big dinner there when the Prime Minister of the day appeared and gave a speech. Anyone remember Brian Mulroney?

At the end of each dinner someone would come along and ask if we wanted to work later and if you said no it was fine and if you said yes it was fine too. No pressure and I only remember once or twice I chose to stay late.

Between the Laurier and the Congress Center I was making some good part-time income. Meanwhile, my course was steaming ahead. I was baking some Black Forest cakes and chocolate éclairs. I used to bring them back and have the Scottish couple I met try them out at their place. They would make dinner and I would supply the dessert.

Outside of a couple of beers with people I worked with, the Scottish couple, and school that was about what I did socially for those four months. Saving some money or just breaking even was all I wanted to do.

I made up my mind that if I passed the basic pastry course in Ottawa, I would go for the advanced course in London, England.

I had to study each recipe so that I knew them all by heart. On exam day we had three hours to prepare a dessert. The difficult part was we didn't know until we came to class that day which dessert was chosen by the teacher for us to prepare.

The Topaz was the one I got and it turned out quite well. The judges looked it over and gave me a good mark. Quite pleased with myself, I was now looking forward to going back to England. I would use the Grandparent Visa like I did back in 1990 to find work. I was making plans to stay at the YMCA in London. Everything seemed set.

Unlike things in the past that I had done, this seemed well orchestrated.

I was sorry to say goodbye to Ottawa and the places I worked. If I wasn't so ambitious, I probably would have stayed a great deal longer and made a go of it there, especially at the Chateau Laurier. That was some hotel!

"Bring on 1993," I thought, being the eternal optimist I was.

1993

After successfully completing the basic pastry course in Ottawa, I was itching to go to London, England to start the advanced pastry segment to get my diploma. Cordon Bleu is world-renowned and I was hoping that by completing both the basic and advanced courses, I could land myself a job in a top-notch kitchen where I could hone my skills. A part of me always wanted to create and I was having a fun time baking. I wasn't a natural at it but I could see my improvement as the course progressed.

Before heading to London I visited my mother during Christmas. She had moved out to Victoria on the west coast that year. She had just finished her contract as housekeeper with this lodge north of Toronto. A friend whom she became close to at this lodge had mentioned to her that she was taking a position with this hotel in Hertfordshire County, England and if I needed to find work and get some practice time in the kitchen to contact her when I arrived overseas. "Fine," I thought, but I had my plans already in place at the YMCA in London. The same sort of living arrangement I had in Ottawa.

On December 26th after a snow delay at Vancouver Airport, I flew 10 hours and touched down at Heathrow Airport ready to go. I had some money and had prepaid my stay at the Y for the first couple of weeks. The course was not due to start till the New Year. In the meantime I was having a blast in London enjoying the sights during that Christmas and New Year break. I saw Peter Ustinov and went to the new (at the time) Barbican Centre on New Year's Day for the Strauss celebration.

My plan was, once I started the course to seek out hotels and restaurants and get some experience in the kitchen and wait on tables. I didn't expect to make a whole lot if I just worked in the kitchen so I had to subsidize my income with some waiting on tables. But then I called my mom and she said this friend of hers was waiting on my call wondering where I was. "Okay," I thought, "I will call her."

After getting off the phone with her, she had convinced me that this job she had was a guarantee and all I had to do was come up and have an interview to meet the manager of the hotel. It was a mere formality, in other words. I could stay at her place until I could find a place of my own.

How I Took a Bartending Course and Traveled for Seventeen Years

So there I was in the heart of London where, you know, there had to be plenty of jobs. But I was going to take the Brit Rail Line about 50 minutes away to Hertfordshire to a place called Ware where someone just pretty much guaranteed that a job was waiting for me. There were pros and cons to the choice. Sure, I could stay in London, but I could see myself running through the money. Actually, looking back, the obvious choice was London, but I made the mistake of taking the acquaintance's offer. I thought at the time this would save me the hassle of looking for someone to take me on, and the thought of working straight away in a kitchen stoked the burn I had to get some work experience. It seemed like the perfect set-up. It made up for the travel time and expense to me to go back and forth to London.

I moved out of the Y and with suitcases in hand took the train to Ware where the woman and her boyfriend met me. Ware was not like London. It is not what you would call a Mecca for tourists. In fact, if you didn't know anyone there, you would have no reason to go there. I had my doubts, but, hey, the job sounded promising.

They had a spare room where I could put my stuff and crash. In a couple of days I would be heading to the manor for the interview. The course was about to begin around the same time. The day of the interview arrived and I was full of optimism.

I want to describe what happened next in a clear concise fashion but that would do what took place no justice. Blue with rage and wanting to strangle this so-called friend of my mom's I will briefly explain what happened.

The interview began and ended in 5 minutes. I was told no hiring would be done till April when they hoped that business would get better. Mentioning that I was told that work would be available and that I displaced myself from the city and moved here all he had to say was he had made no promises and that he was sorry.

"What the heck just happened?" I asked my mom's so-called good friend. All she had to say was she was surprised. *Surprised!!* Now to that day my mom called her "a friend" but if that was my mom's good friend, I'd hate to see her enemies. I gave my mom a lecture for being led on and of course gave myself a beating for trusting a stranger.

So with that, the fun really began. Stuck in Ware, I hit all the personnel agencies. There were signs saying they needed waiters to hire but all they really wanted to do was pad their applicant base. I got one-night jobs in catering.

One place I was a waiter and the way they used to set their tables was leave them bare and once the order was taken you would put the appropriate cutlery down. On more than one occasion I was a dishwasher and pot washer. I relied on lifts to and from work with the older retired ladies that worked on call for any banquet or catering functions that would come up.

I was barely making any ends meet while taking the train into London 2-3 times a week to complete the course. While in London, I would look for work, but without living close by I was not a good prospect to hire.

Then I was told to leave by my mother's so-called "good friend." Fine, but where was I to go?

I ended up finding a place with room and board. Breakfast and dinner was included and I could watch all the *East Enders* episodes I could in the evening. It wasn't cheap either.

I was in a spot where you know everything was set up nicely and then one thing happened and it all changed after that. My Master Card balance was growing. Now it was just a matter of finishing the course.

Amazingly, with all the distraction I finished 4th on the final exam. We all had to make a Sacher Torte. My butter cream was to die for and it was one of those things that either you get right or screw up every time. I happened to be real good at making butter cream.

I graduated, but due to my debt load and living expense, I never again ventured into the kitchen. I still have the recipes on paper that is changing colours as the years fly by. Soon they will be merely scribble notes on paper like a papyrus from the ancient Egyptian civilizations. What a shame that was the whole series of events to start off my second time in England.

I was in survival mode. The room was situated in Rye House right beside Ware. I needed to find some full-time work. At this point, I had decided to look locally. Just cut down on the expense of travelling on the train and work near Rye House. I thought about drinking lots of Rye Whiskey, too, but that would have made me go deeper in debt. Rye and Rye House, get it?

I found a full-time job working in a parts plant right after the course. My job was taking these steel parts and putting them at a certain angle under this press machine to bend them all to fit whatever they were going to be used for. Lucky I didn't lose any fingers doing this but that is what I did. I worked overtime on Saturdays as a machine operator and that was a higher pay. In fact, the bosses were so impressed with my work that they wanted to hire me as a full time machine operator.

After I had worked about five weeks I began to ask myself if this was where I was going to end up? A machine operator living in Rye House?

I remember doing a lot of walking to the train station in the morning, going two stops then getting off and walking to work. After eight hours of doing the same thing, back to the room and board spot I lived. I made sure I always had the latest edition of the *Hotel and Catering* magazine so I could jump back into the hospitality industry. It wouldn't be easy for me to find that job. It had to be where I could save money and pay off the debt I had accumulated, again.

There was this one ad that intrigued me. Interviews were being held in Ipswich for the Island Hotel on Tresco in the Isles of Scilly. They were looking for a head waiter, so I called the number and was told the following Saturday they would be conducting interviews. I got an afternoon interview so I had time to get there.

How I Took a Bartending Course and Traveled for Seventeen Years

I got myself all psyched up and took a couple of trains to Ipswich. The hotel and the dining room manager met me. "I really need this job," I thought, so I had to nail the interview.

The interview went like a charm and a few days later I got the confirmation that I had the job. The time to go would be a couple of weeks later, which brought me to the beginning of May.

The real cool thing was how I left the plants factory. I worked the next week and a half but throughout the remaining time I would tell people that I would be leaving soon. You see, everyone hated working in this place. Then people would start asking me when would it be that I was going to leave. I wouldn't tell but I would say, "you will know soon." I had everyone waiting for the big moment.

It was on a Thursday that I decided to leave. I mentioned to a few co-workers that that day at three, when our break happened I was going into the office and handing my resignation in. They were aghast! "Really?" they said, "you are leaving!"

I said my goodbyes beforehand, then when the buzzer went at three I trotted into the office and announced that I was leaving at the end of the day to move on to what I was born to do and that was be in a restaurant serving food. They were on the one hand sad I was leaving because they had big plans for me, but happy I was pursuing something I enjoyed. I was quite a popular guy there, as a lot of the employees had never travelled too far. I was a bit of an anomaly, you could say.

Once again, I was happy to be moving on.

Off to the Isles of Scilly

On the Saturday I moved out with my bags from the boarder house I was living in at the time. I thanked the woman for the meals and bedding. She was happy to hear the news when it happened. She knew I needed to get back in the restaurant industry.

I took the train to Penzance situated on the southwest coast of England where I stayed in a bed and breakfast for a couple of days. From there, I grabbed the helicopter that would take me to the island of Saint Mary's. Then it was a water taxi to the island of Tresco.

The islands were out in the North Atlantic, so swimming was out of the question. The water was cold. If you took the two-hour ride aboard the ship that brought the supplies to the islands, you were sure to get seasick. With no stabilizers and rough seas, many people would be heaving it as they travelled. I witnessed a lot of green faces getting off the ship when I did see it arrive in port in St. Mary's.

The island of Tresco was quite unique. There were no roads, therefore no cars, so to get around there were these cattle trails. It was like England many years ago. The families who resided there were a bit strange too. They all looked a bit peculiar with all the family incest that was probably going on due to the lack of choice. There wasn't a lot to do for the year-round inhabitants. A little sheep grazing and pub-crawling were the options. It was a beautiful spot though and an oasis of tranquility for those vacationers who wanted to escape the rat race.

The hotel was nice. I had the staff accommodation provided for and the work conditions were quite good. I volunteered amongst the three of us who were the leaders in the dining room to work the breakfast shift on most occasions.

Working breakfast was quite different from what I was used to, though, and because of that I didn't like it at all. In North America, I was used to having someone order their breakfast and it arrived at their table all at once. A refill of coffee with the bill in hand would end the service.

Unfortunately, it didn't go that easy here. They would order their breakfast and it was like serving a buffet to their table. Maybe they would start with fresh fruit so you would call for a plate of fresh fruit to the kitchen. Deliver it and when they were finished, order their kippers and when that was over, then their bacon and eggs and blood pudding. It was like you were constantly running back and forth to the kitchen serving three course breakfasts to the guests. People would just be gobbling their food down and waiting for the next course to arrive. When it got really busy you were just running your butt off. Then the juices, flavoured steeped teas, and coffees on top. It was more stressful than it needed to be. I hated it.

The management saw that I wasn't too used to this English style so they gave me the job of being in charge of wine service during dinner, which I enjoyed much more. I helped out during the day in the restaurant but my main focus was back in the evening. I enjoyed my nights as the closer sitting down with the night bartender quaffing some pints of Boddingtons Ale. On my day off, I would usually head to Saint Mary's to walk through the old city and have a lunch.

Staff meals were provided for, but I could not name one that became a favourite, as they were all pretty bad. Pete Townsend of the Who came by for a visit one day and so did the Earl who owned Tresco. A very nice chap, he was.

It was beautiful but isolated. The water was too cold to swim in but I did one day much to everyone's disbelief. There was a huge party the night before. These South Africans brewed up some Ginger Beer to drink. All I remember was drinking this and waking up the next morning with a humongous headache.

I was off that day, thankfully, but I had to get rid of the hangover. What I did was walk out to my chest in the water. The bystanders thought I was nuts. Ten minutes later after having dunked my whole body in, head to toe, I walked out and the hangover was gone. To this day, I tell people to get rid of a hangover by taking a cold shower. It worked for me that day.

Every time I would get paid I would send money to the bank to pay my credit card down.

Coincidentally, I found out Regina Renaissance was stopping by and sending people on a tender over to Tresco for a shore excursion. I couldn't miss this. Lo and behold, I saw Mike the maître d' whom I worked with on the same ship the year before.

Shocked when he saw me, he asked me what the heck I was doing there. It was the last place he ever thought he would see me. I explained what happened and he said, "Listen, I am calling the office in Fort Lauderdale and telling them you are going to call. Get back on the ship." I thought about it for a bit and decided that would be a great idea. Would they hire me back, though?

The next day I got to the phone and called Fort Lauderdale. They remembered me and asked me when I wanted to come back and where I would like to go, which was pretty nice of them. I said the Caribbean and they gave me a date at the beginning of October to be aboard Renaissance 5 in Antigua.

They were delighted and so was I. Now I was returning to make some serious coin and put another England adventure behind me.

Nothing Ever Comes Easy

At the time I left Tresco I had paid off my debt and had some money on hand. It seemed like up till now in my life there were times I had some money and other times I was paying off some debt. But outside of the paying off debt part, I was enjoying the single life and getting around to different places.

Getting reacquainted with former Renaissance Cruise Line ex-co-workers was a signal to get back to working on the ships. It was a fluke that the ship's itinerary included a stop at the hotel I was working in and their insistence that I get back to the ship had me eager to return. I had until the beginning of October when I reported for duty, so naturally, I wanted to travel around.

First I wanted to visit this girl in Switzerland who was the Swedish girl I stayed with back in Sweden. She was working a season in Switzerland at the time. Then I had plans on going to Germany and then back to England. It was going to be a great trip. I had accommodations everywhere, so it was not going to be that expensive.

My last night at the Island Hotel I partied so much that the next day on the boat taxi to Saint Mary's I was heaving it over the side at the back. After the helicopter flight, I stopped by the B&B I stayed at before heading over to Tresco to see if they wouldn't mind keeping some stuff for me until I got back in a few weeks time. They were real nice and said, "Sure, it will be right here waiting for you."

So off to London I went on the overnight train. When I arrived in London I would head directly to the bus terminal and grab the bus to Lyon, France. From Lyon I took another bus to Geneva. Finally, I'd take a train, then another bus up this mountain to where this girl was working. I don't remember how long off the top the bus ride took, but I do remember getting off at Lyon and standing outside waiting for our connection. It felt like I was living in Lyon and just taking local transit. It was a weird feeling.

Anyhow, I finally get to Geneva to get on the train. I got off at a stop I had passed by many times while I worked in Switzerland. Then I took the bus up the mountain to this small mountain resort. I see the girl and her boyfriend, she didn't tell me about. Also a lot of other guys she never told me about. Hmmm... I thought maybe I read more into this than I should have. I think between the time we had a beer together and the following morning we saw one another about an hour. When she took off the next day with her boyfriend in his Corvette I left her a goodbye note and headed to my next stop. So much for that!

My next place to visit was Germany in a town called Kisslegg. There was an Irish girl and a German whom I worked with in Switzerland who had married and were running a restaurant. It was his room with a view I lived in after he went of to work in China.

In Kisslegg they had a really nice restaurant and already a couple of young children. She was the active one during the day so while he worked we went out for a bicycle ride to a park where there was a swing set.

Well, we started to swing away. I happened to mention that when I was younger we used to have these jump contests on who could jump the farthest off the swing. She dared me to jump. I said no way until when she turned around I decided to jump quickly. The sudden decision to jump was not planned well.

I was tumbling and afraid that I was going to hit my head so I put up my arm to block the impact. My right wrist landed the wrong way instead. I looked at it and I think my face turned green. My stomach turned nauseous and I was yelling expletives.

She came over and had a look and asked if I could move my hands and fingers. I was only able to move a finger. My wrist was bent.

I said, "Maybe I just sprained it."

She started laughing and said, "I don't think so."

I rode the bicycle back with one hand and when we get to her place I lay down hoping that this was all a bad dream. It was not really sore, but the wrist looked real ugly.

A nurse who was eating in the restaurant that night came up and looked at it. She told me I better go to the hospital and get it checked out. It was probably broken.

This is something I did not need! It was about six to seven weeks from now that I would be starting on the ship.

The next morning, after I slept with it, we headed to the hospital. It was a Sunday and there were not too many people on staff. Her husband came with me to act as translator. The doctor, who had to be in his mid-twenties, came in and I told him what happened.

He took this tension bar and attached to each finger a device that would ensure the fingers were tense when he started straightening the wrist out. Turning this wheel, he straightened the wrist to take an x-ray.

There was a panel on the wall, so when the picture was taken, I could see what the problem was. Yes, it was broken in two places. We had to wait for the anesthesiologist to arrive. "It might take a couple of hours," the doctor told me.

So we chatted amongst ourselves while waiting. I think we were the only ones in the hospital on that beautiful Sunday. Finally, I asked him if he knew what he was doing. He said, "Sure, why wouldn't I?"

"Well, I am getting tired of waiting for this guy to inject me with something to deaden the pain. Why can't we just go ahead and put the bone together and set the cast on?" I asked. They start laughing.

Then they stopped laughing when they realized I was dead serious. I asked what it was he had to do. He replied that he had to do this like this and that like that and then put the cast on. "Okay," I said, "when you put the bone in place, just tell me before you do it and I will yell at that exact moment. Count to three then I will yell and you snap it back."

The doctor and my friend were telling me it would hurt doing it like that. "I know," I said, "but if I yell it will be like a karate guy breaking boards. The yell will deaden the pain."

The doctor told my friend to leave the room. Without going in greater detail, the doctor put the bones back in place without fail the first time and put the cast on.

He then told me I needed the cast on for six weeks. Just two days before I was reporting to the ship. Now, did I call the ship or not to tell them? "No sweat," I thought, "I will be ready. I am not going to bother."

Fortunately as well it was all covered under the EEC health plan. I was a United Kingdom resident at the time paying UK taxes and in possession of a British Health Card.

I called to an end the holiday. Not before I went to the Oktoberfest in Munich for some pints though. I bought a cheap ticket back home, which at this time was Montreal. Before flying out I called the B&B in Penzance to tell them what happened and that I wouldn't be around to collect my stuff. I asked if they would store it for me till the next time I was in town. Probably after my next contract I would be back.

"Sure," they said. There wasn't much, but I left some cooking knives and books with them that I didn't want to part with at the time. I was always a travelling bed of knowledge. My luggage was always heavy because of the books I carried around.

So I flew home with the cast. I rented a room out in this house for a couple of months on the Lakeshore in Montreal. It was cumbersome living with the cast and I couldn't work, so all I did was do a lot of walking and reading. I ate sparingly in cheap restaurants all the time squeezing a rubber ball thinking that when the cast came off I would be as good as new.

Now, being outside of Canada for quite a while my Healthcare Card had expired, so technically I had no insurance at all for doctor or hospital visits. Even to get the cast off it was going to cost me big dollars. My old family doctor in Lachine was still around, so I popped in to see him to explain my predicament.

The following Thursday it would be six weeks. I had to get the cast off because on the Saturday I was flying out to the ship.

He told me to go to Lachine General at noon. He was going to be there and would find me at patient check-in. There he would sneak me in a back room to saw my cast off. I thanked him a lot.

Well, as planned he started to saw the cast off with the machine and as he was doing it, my face was turning green and my head was spinning. The cast came off and he said it looked fine.

Well to me it didn't, because I couldn't move my wrist!! Then he said, "Of course not," and added I needed to go for physiotherapy.

Therapy! There I was supposed to be waiting on tables in Antigua back on the ship that coming Saturday.

It was pretty naïve of me to think I could just walk away when the cast came off able to use my hand in a normal fashion. So I squeezed that rubber ball and tried moving my wrist around as much as I could, hoping that some miracle would occur in the two days before I was to start my six-month contract with the ship.

To make things worse, the ticket they sent to me was ridiculous. It started off with a 7 AM flight to Pittsburgh, where I spent a couple of hours walking around their nice new airport at the time. Then it was about 11 AM that I had a flight to Miami where I spent another couple of hours sitting around a bar working that rubber ball in the palm of my right hand. Still hoping by some miracle my wrist would gain mobility.

After that I took a short flight to Puerto Rico, where we were not allowed off the plane until we took off for Antigua. I cannot remember, to this day, if I made it on time to do the pool deck barbeque that night, but I do remember going to the pier-side with the rest of the waiters. The hotel manager Jose came over and asked me if something was wrong with my wrist. I said it was okay and that I had just sprained it a few days earlier.

So it was with great difficulty that I worked with one good hand. Fortunately, my tray-carrying arm was on my good left side. When it came time to lower my tray of eight plates with cloches down on the side stand, it was like watching it done in slow motion every time. Bending down gingerly to keep the tray straight, I held it from the side with my limp wrist. This was quite the task. No major accident occurred and as for placing cups and saucers down, I would put them down with my right hand, which was supported by my healthy left hand. I would just cradle show plates in my arm and put them gently on their spot on the table.

It was tedious, to say the least, but I survived. Five weeks later and after much exercise in the warm waters of the Caribbean, my wrist gained strength and I was back to normal.

Cruising the Caribbean and Crossing the Atlantic 1994

We hit most of the islands of the Caribbean with my favourite being St. Bart's. My least favourite was the island of St. Thomas, which was the only U.S. Port we docked in. There we had loading, which would take up most of your free time. Throw in lifeboat drill and maybe we had an hour or two tops free time. The real pain was lunch service, which was usually pretty busy.

That was because the passengers never liked the food ashore as much as the big buffets at lunch. Why bother eating ashore when you can eat all you want on the ship. All they would do is shop and lay on the beach for a while. Then they'd come back on board. It was a tough contract.

What I came to realize is many people never went ashore at all. They just wanted to eat and eat and eat.

The cruise I will never forget was during Christmas that year. The cruise was full of vacationers from New York. From 7:30 to 9:30, breakfast was served, but they would all arrive at 9:25, so we couldn't start taking down the buffet till at least 10 o'clock.

The worst time was when we had the beach barbeque on Virgin Gorda. The island and setting was idyllic. I was chosen that day to work the lunch on board. This was usually a fantastic opportunity to go ashore later and just kick back without having to worry about bringing all the stuff back to the ship after it was all over. The lunch was scheduled from noon to one and the passengers expected to stay on board numbered about a half dozen. These were people who for medical or physical reasons couldn't go ashore and eat.

Lunch started and the hotel manager started to hear that they were unhappy with the barbeque and wanted to eat in the dining room. About 30 came back and lunch didn't end till four. The dining room was set up for dinner, except for those couple of tables we needed for lunch, so it was like serving two dinners that day. It was brutal. They all ordered New York Steaks. By the time dinner rolled around a couple of hours later, I was a train wreck wondering what the heck just happened. A couple of waiters were called back from the beach to help me out. But most were resting by four when I was still running around. I don't think I was back to the cabin till about 4:45 that afternoon. When they disembarked that Saturday the whole crew napped. No one hit the beach. Exhaustion reigned throughout the ship.

There were not a lot of young passengers contrary to other bigger cruise ships. There was a joke one cruise when the maître d' mentioned that there was a passenger who was 38 on the ship. We said, "Wow," and he chimed back that she was born in '38!

Another strange thing happened: my feet grew two sizes to size 15. I don't know whether it was the humidity or what, but I was unable to wear my shoes during dinner service, so I had to wear black-laced running shoes. Shoes my size are difficult to find in the Tropics as most of the islanders shoe sizes are small compared to Northern countries. It was a challenge to walk on my feet as it always felt I was walking on nails. Very uncomfortable that was. My contract began with a bad wrist and was ending with bad feet.

The Transatlantic crossing in the spring of 1994 began in Martinique, went to Madeira, then on to Lisbon. It was as calm as could be during the crossing. There were only about 60 or so passengers on board, so it was a real easy cruise. I even witnessed a man overboard safety drill.

That all changed, however, when we got to Las Palmas in the Canary Islands. Before we left port, the crew was told to close the portholes as we were heading into rough sea. We were just starting dinner service when we left port and you heard loud bangs everywhere. The waves were thunderous! You had to secure your dishes on the side stand and when your back waiter came out with seven salads for the table, usually you would have a few left over as people were getting seasick all over the place. The entire seven-day cruise we hit only one port in Morocco. The winds were bad and I remember looking out at the front of the ship and the bow was almost going right in the water. The ship was small and had less than 10,000 gross tons. Compared to the ships nowadays, this ship was tiny, so it really felt the effect of the high waves.

I got seasick, as did most of the crew. Passengers wanted their money back, but no one gets a refund because of the weather. You would be lying down in your bunk bed and sliding up and down in it due to the motion of the ocean. That was the worst seas I ever encountered while working on the ship. There were other times, but none lasted for the entire cruise like that experience.

We did a lot of ports in the Mediterranean for the next couple of months before my contract ended at the end of May, beginning of June. I met a waiter from Croatia who had a place in Myrtle Beach and invited me to come over to stay with him and his wife. It sounded good and after what transpired during the cruise I could use some time on the beach. I left the ship in Athens and flew home to Montreal to see what was going on and catch up on some news.

The only other noteworthy thing took place one time in St. Thomas when an au pair from Iceland was holidaying with her American family from

Virginia. The family had rented a sailboat and was in the area the same day I was probably doing loading in St. Thomas. She took a picture of Renaissance 5 and probably thought that maybe one day it would be a neat thing to work on a ship. Little did I know, or did she know at the time that one day our lives would cross paths.

But now it was the summer of 1994 and time for Myrtle Beach!

Living the Dream

I loved Myrtle Beach since I was a kid when we used to go there on family holidays. It is a Mecca for Canadian tourists with its beautiful beach and fun things to do all day long and well into the evening.

It was the beginning of June, just before the vacationers would all come in swarms to fill up the hotel rooms. I had the phone number and address of the waiter and gave him a call to let him know what day I would be arriving.

I was always one to take up an offer from someone no matter how well I knew that person. If anything, all it did was get me to that place and if the offer was not available any longer, then I had to scramble to find other means to stay there. By this time, my whole life experience up to that point had served me well in handling sudden changes of plan. If everything seemed to go well I was always wondering when things were going to change. Arriving in Myrtle Beach was just another example of finding an alternate plan.

My waiter friend picked me up at the airport and I could tell he was a bit stressed out. Apparently, him and his new wife were not hitting it off very well and there was a young child in the mix. I said, "Listen, if this is a bad time, I have to find a place fast before everything gets booked up." He helped me out and I ended finding this hotel room with a fridge, stove and, of course, AC for a real good price. I never saw him again, but he did leave me with a VIP pass to one of the nightclubs in town, which was just dandy.

My lifestyle for two months was sublime. The hotel was situated a couple of blocks up from the beach. My schedule each day went something like the following. I would get up about 8:30 and go to the newspaper box and pick up the Myrtle Beach newspaper. Then make myself a coffee and sit outside and read the headlines. Then about an hour later go to the restaurant for the $1.99 breakfast where the charming waitress provided a thermos of coffee for me. At about eleven I would head to the beach where I would stay till three. Head back to the hotel and have a shower then hit the bar for happy hour, which started at 4.

Happy hours were great that summer. One afternoon I arrived at the bar and saw a white Bronco being followed by a few police cruisers. Everyone was glued to the television witnessing OJ making a run for it. I couldn't believe it! The greatest all time rushing leader up to that day. He had been the only one to rush for more than 2000 yards in one season. Now I was watching him make the run of his life.

The Vancouver Canucks hockey team was in the Stanley Cup Final against the Rangers that year and it went the full 7 games before New York won their first cup in 50 years. I watched the Houston Rockets win the NBA title and the World Cup Soccer tournament was held for the first time in the United States that year.

I was always a bit starved for lack of sports while working on the ship, so to see all these events and OJ on the run like that made for an entertaining stay. The nightclub was great and I got into line dancing which was the rage back then.

I wrote a letter to the Bed and Breakfast in Penzance back in England where my stuff was being stored to say that I wouldn't be there until 1995 to pick it up. I never got a reply back, of course. For all I knew the place could have burned down, but right now I couldn't care less.

My dream at that moment was to work on the ships for as long as I could so that in a few years I would be making my home in Myrtle Beach. The lifestyle suited me and with plenty to do down there I would never get bored. The girls were plentiful as well. Finally, I figured out where I wanted to live and I figured the rest would fall into place quite seamlessly. I had set some goals for a change.

Another Setback

With that thought in mind, I headed back home to Montreal to await my ticket to Athens, where I would board Renaissance 4. It was going to be exciting. We were going to do the Mediterranean Cruises between Istanbul, Turkey and Piraeus in Greece and also between Civitavecchia in Italy and Barcelona. Then later on in the contract, we would be doing the six-week crossing from Piraeus near Athens to Singapore. This was going to be a great contract, I thought.

I was becoming very well-known on the ship. Now when I returned, I always met people I had worked with on a previous contract. This was my third contract and I was planning on doing a lot more.

The contract started off very well. I was at the top of my game and having the time of my life then something went terribly wrong.

Every few weeks on a rotation basis we were assigned to work behind the buffet during breakfast and lunch. This meant setting up the buffet by moving chairs out into the hallway so we could clear Tables one and two. Then I would decorate the buffet the night before and put the plates on so that all I had to do in the morning was bring the food out from the kitchen and set it up nicely on the buffet. Light the sternos underneath the chafing dishes for the hot feature on the buffet and be ready to go.

Throughout the week for some odd reason my back started really hurting right down my leg. Midway through the cruise, my back started to seize on me so badly I couldn't stand anymore. In fact, I was so bad that in order to loosen it up, the Polish doctor was pouncing on my back just so he could get a crack in it. Nothing worked. One afternoon, I was so bad that it took me 15 minutes just to find a way to get out of my top bunk and crawl down the hallway to see the doctor. I missed three dinner shifts, which usually resulted in the cruise line simply sending you home.

On a ship you cannot be sick, and if you are, they have to replace you with a healthy person very quickly. A man short, especially at dinner service, is real difficult to replace, as we worked in teams of two with no replacement should anyone go down.

It was diagnosed as a bad sciatica nerve and quite literally it took me down. I was only a couple of weeks away from heading to Asia and I had to be flown home unfit to work. Here I was, 35 years old and in the past couple of years I had broken my wrist, had feet trouble, and now was experiencing back trouble. I began to wonder if it would be a good idea now just to say goodbye to the ship life. It was taking a toll on my body.

Back to Canada

So it was from Istanbul four months into the contract that I was flying home with a bad sciatic nerve causing me severe pain. I remember the hard landing in Montreal after having sat on the plane for a long stretch and feeling the pain shoot up my back when the wheels touched ground. It was November of 1994.

I called up my Scottish friends in Ottawa who had just moved into a house an hour outside of Ottawa close to Smith Falls. She was a physiotherapist, which I didn't know about, so they invited me to stay with them. She would help me do some easy stretching exercises on a daily basis and just take it easy with some walks during the day. When she saw me she could see I was in bad shape.

After very little thought, I quickly let the ship know I wanted to return in about six weeks' time. During that time, I received some compensation from the company, which was a pittance really, but it did provide me with some spending money. While staying with my Scottish friends, I was witness to a few séances. They conducted séances with others to bring back spirits of lost family members and they saw the future and other interesting things. They earned a living this way as well as working at some part-time jobs.

During the time I was there, they were still waiting for their Canadian visas. They asked me for a loan of $1000 Canadian dollars to further their visa application. I didn't know much about it but they needed the money and I was happy they could help me get better and give me a place to crash at the same time.

They promised they would pay me back but when I left I lost contact with them. I heard they had split up and had gone separate ways. I had lots of money so it didn't matter.

The only thing I didn't like about them not keeping in contact was I met this girl while I was there who I took a fancy to and I wanted to see her again but that was through them, so it never went any further. Later on, we did exchange a letter or two, but as things happened someone else would soon replace her. Anyway, I couldn't see going back to Ottawa in the near future. There was too much else to do.

Now healthy and ready to head back to the ship, I went out to Victoria B.C. to visit Mom again. As mentioned, she had moved there a couple of years earlier. I thought it would be good to visit during the Christmas season before heading back. I phoned Renaissance Cruises and much to my relief found out my chance to go to Asia had not vanished. They said I could join another ship that would be arriving in Singapore shortly. The flight they bought for me was ridiculous. They had me flying from Vancouver to Toronto. Then from Toronto to London and then I would be there for eleven hours before grabbing a flight from London to Kuala Lumpur in Malaysia. Then it was an hour there without leaving the 747 then on to Jakarta, Indonesia where I was going to get on the ship.

So it was 15 time zones over three days you could say. Instead of flying me west over the Pacific I was taking the world tour going East!

I arrived in Jakarta and I could see in the distance past customs the agent holding up the sign indicating to me he was the one to take me to the ship. Except there was one problem. The immigration officer wanted a bribe to let me through. He wanted my ring and watch! I said no way. He told the port agent to go away and I was deported out of the country! Now, I showed him the contract in his office, but it wasn't good enough. He wanted me to call head office, but I didn't have the number in Fort Lauderdale handy. Besides, it was the middle of the night back in Florida.

So that same British Airways 747 that got me there I was sent back on. I was hustled back on the plane with my suitcase, just making it before they closed the luggage hatch and took off. No ticket, no nothing. I had just flown 17 hours from London and now I was returning. There was another crew-member from another cruise line who suffered the same fate as I. The stewardesses knew what happened and they felt so sorry for us. They gave us free shots from the bar.

I got hammered and fell asleep part of the way back to London. I remember the turbulence during the flight. Watching those wings flex in the wind I think had me heaving once or twice. I saw *Merry Christmas Mr. Bean* four times and *Forrest Gump* twice! When I arrived in London, I explained what had happened and they put me on a flight from London directly back to Vancouver.

We landed in Vancouver and my name was announced to see the steward upon disembarking the jet. He asked me who was going to pay for this flight. I said call Renaissance Cruises and gave them the phone number. I had had enough. Tired and not having showered in a few days and travelling through 30 time zones there and back I just wanted to head back to Victoria.

Two funny things happened along the way. One was I had the same waitress at Heathrow asking me what the hell happened on my way back from Jakarta and the other was that my mother had already mailed me two letters since I left only a few days ago. Needless to say, when I knocked on the door she was a bit surprised.

I was a bit fed up so I decided to set some roots. I wasn't sure I wanted to return to the ship after all this. I had the injury and this experience plus now I was heading toward my 36th birthday in a couple of months and I started to think I had to start thinking about planting my feet somewhere. All this travelling was getting to be too much. I didn't call back Fort Lauderdale to tell them what happened. I just rented out an apartment and signed a lease. It was a tiny bachelor. The rent was $435 a month.

A few days passed before Renaissance Cruises called and asked me what happened. I told them and they said that would be the last time they take crew on in Jakarta. But would I like to join the same ship I left with the bad sciatic when it arrived in Singapore on January 1st? I took maybe a couple of seconds to think about it and after getting reassurances that Singapore would be much more professional than the Jakarta experience, I said sure. It was going to be via London again, but this time a direct flight from Vancouver and then direct from London to Singapore with a small stopover at Heathrow. Not the 11-hour wait I had the week before.

Beautiful Asia - 1995

It was pretty exciting touching down in Singapore on New Year's Day 1995.

There was no problem clearing customs and I was picked up by the port agent without delay and went off to the ship. Unlike a couple of other contracts on board, I encountered no health issues during this six-month contract.

They were 10-day voyages that started off in Singapore and ended up in Bali, Indonesia. Some of the stops in between were Lombok and Jakarta. In Lombok we headed to this hotel and jumped around in their pool while in Jakarta we headed to the Hard Rock Café.

Indonesia was pretty amazing. The islands we visited were lush with vegetation and the people were really friendly. The beaches were fantastic and it was always hot and humid. I like the humidity, to be honest, as even here at home when the humidity starts to disappear toward the tail end of summer I notice how much cooler it feels.

There was the island of Komodo where we saw the Komodo dragons up close. One time the ship went off its normal itinerary and we hit a lot of different obscure places. On my 36th birthday I remember going for a ride on a rickshaw in Ujung Pandang on the island of Sulawesi.

Seeing the zoo in Semarang on the island of Java was interesting, as, being in that part of the world, I had the opportunity to see a whole bunch of different animals. In Semarang I always went for massages that were a mere ten dollars. The girls use to walk on your back and find the spot that needed a good crack. I loved going to that place.

Borobudur, an ancient Buddhist temple from the 9th century was something to see.

The ship always came close to the volcanic island Krakatau in the Sunda Strait between Java and Sumatra. This volcano was always spewing ash even when we were there. It erupted first back in the late 1800s. We got real close one time and I was outside on the lower deck looking at this mountain. As I was gazing at it I saw this big fish jump out of the water about two feet and just when it did there was this loud bang and the ash was flying out of the top. I guess this fish felt it was going to happen the way it jumped out of the water.

How I Took a Bartending Course and Traveled for Seventeen Years

Bali was always embarkation day so it was pretty busy for the crew, but we managed to head into town or to the beach that day.

Singapore was another spot that had plenty to see and do. We used to get our provisions that day so loading, took a fair chunk of the morning, but in the afternoon we managed to check out the Raffles Hotel—famous for introducing that Singapore Sling to the world.

We started the five-week voyage back to the Mediterranean mid-March with stops in such places as Kuala Lumpur in Malaysia. The first shock someone gets when they are heading ashore is the sign that reads anyone caught with drugs will be sentenced to death. Not that I took drugs, but I quickly realized these people meant business. We toured the city looking at the skyscrapers that were going up all around.

Then it was off to Phuket, Thailand where Nigel the Bartender challenged us all to go bungee jumping at Tarzan's Bungee Jump. He got about 10 of us to go. It was a jump of 50-meters from a crane. I wasn't too keen on it, but after a few beers and everyone daring the other to jump it didn't take me long to go for it.

When this waiter from the States did it I had to do it. He went first and I went second. It was the wildest thing I ever did in my life. When I jumped there was two to three seconds of free falling when there is no sound. All you feel is a mix of terror and exhilaration.

When I was shot back up with the elastic cord, the blood was going to my head and it felt like my eyeballs were going to pop out. I am glad I did it, but whether I would do it again I am not sure. I was single then, but now that I am married I don't think my wife would let me do it.

In Bombay we saw where Gandhi lived for a while in this house now turned into a museum. The ship docked near the Gateway of India, which was a tall monument close by the Taj Mahal Hotel. Around the monument were the peddlers and snake charmers trying to get their reptiles and animals to do tricks for money. The hotel right beside all this provided a stark contrast between the rich and poor. In Bombay, the poor lived on the streets in tents. Laundry was done outside in this big area and hung to dry. Cars honked everywhere.

In the tourist resort of Goa in India we headed to the beach but decided not to swim as the sign said swim at your own risk. Was it because of the sharks or the pollution? I wasn't quite sure, so we stayed out of the water.

I remember on the Indian Ocean heading to the crew deck to do some sunbathing and looking over the sides of the hull at the keel of the ship. I saw about 15 dolphins swimming effortlessly alongside, toying with us, slowing down and then speeding up.

After India we hit other ports. Dubai was a great overnight. I saw a singer that not only sounded like Joe Cocker, but looked like him too.

In Jeddah, Saudi Arabia, I won the draw to go on a tour around the city with the other passengers on a bus. Talk about unbelievably clean. They take all their scrap metal and make designs out of them throughout the city.

I went to the Salalah Beach Resort in Oman to lie on the beach there and shopped around in Muscat the capital city. We also hit the port of Aden in Yemen where you felt like you were a bit unwelcome. It was where the USS Cole was bombed a few years later.

Then it was off to the Red Sea and ports like Sharm el Sheikh in Egypt, which is quite a resort for those living in that part of the world.

After returning to the Mediterranean and seeing places I had seen already in previous cruises plus a few others, I wrapped up a truly memorable six months.

On April 12th of 1995 the girl who saw Renaissance 5 in St. Thomas the previous year while being an au pair in the States got on board the ship in Monte Carlo. I happened to be at the Purser's Desk when she arrived. I took note of the new stewardess and left to the dining room, not taking too much notice at the time.

Of course I had an interest in girls, as always, but jeopardizing my freedom was a price I didn't want to pay at the time. I was having too much fun. Or was it because I was getting close to settling? I could feel myself caving in under the relentless pressure all around me of working with beautiful women everywhere. I was not a playboy and I knew if I relented that would be it for me.

Missing the Ship and My Biggest Complaint

There are some things that, when they happen, appear really bad but later on it turns out all right. You know when you miss an appointment or the bus leaves without you. Well try missing the ship you work on!

I had a crush on this bar server from Sweden. She was much younger than I was, which actually wasn't new because nearly everyone I liked up to this time was a lot younger. It seemed like I had this yearning to meet someone from Sweden too and move there.

In fact, Sweden is one of those countries that remind me a lot of Canada. There are tons of trees and taking the train ride from Goteborg to Stockholm reminded me a lot of the train ride I often took when I was a kid between Montreal and Toronto. Even when the ship was heading into Stockholm it was like you were going through the St. Lawrence Seaway just outside of Montreal with the cottages lined along the shore only with the Swedish flag instead of a Canadian one

Unfortunately for me or fortunately, depending on how you look at it, this girl wasn't as interested in me as she was in the captain of the ship. The captain knew I liked her too. Our rapport had developed during my first contract with Renaissance but it evaporated as time passed. His going out with a girl he knew I had eyes on made things pretty tense. Never mess with the captain's girl or things can be made quite uncomfortable.

It felt especially frosty when I was serving the captain's table during the farewell gala and the soufflés were running a couple of minutes late. It is normal for the Captain to want to get the heck away from all the stupid questions the people around the table are asking him each and every cruise, but when it was me serving his table and the soufflés were running behind time, his evil look was even more sharp.

So when his four-month stint as Captain was finally coming to an end, I figured there was my chance. I didn't care if she was in love with him or not, I was going to wing it and see what would happen.

She had a week to go and I could feel she was buckling under the pressure I was putting on her. There was a chance in Sorrento, Italy that I could perhaps take her out to lunch and take it from there. She said sure, she would love to go and so we took the tender ashore.

We were having a nice lunch and I figured I was in like flint that night. We headed to pick up the last tender to the ship that we thought was departing at 5:00. We arrived at the spot where we thought the tender would be waiting for us to take us to the ship. But much to our surprise the last tender had already left!

Looking in the distance, I noticed the ship with smoke coming out of the funnel, making its way out to sea. You know that feeling when you know something just happened and you get that sinking feeling in your gut!

Now this girl I was with starts panicking. She is almost in tears. Not so much she has missed the tender but if this gets back to her boyfriend the captain that she was with me missing the ship, there would go her chance to live in Tuscany the rest of her life!

But I had other ideas. I figured I only had a short time left on my contract and thought I would probably not be returning to the ship the next time around so should I run and find the ship agent or just wait a minute and let her panic some more. Heck, we could always take the train to Taormina and catch the ship the next day!

Well I quickly did the right thing and got a hold of the guy with the walkie talkie and told him that was our ship out there and we are crew that should be on board. He mumbles a swear word under his breath as we show him our crew cards and he calls the ship. On the phone you could tell there was just crackle then I could hear the captain mumble something not so nice on the other end. Like, all I could think about was that I was sure to be fired. It was a good run, but that was it for me. However, I had one good thing going, and that was that the person I was with was the other captain's girlfriend.

So we were taxied out to the waiting ship. The passengers are laughing and clapping on deck as we pulled up. She was hiding her head while I was there sort of smirking and waving back. The ladder came down and we climbed aboard. We were escorted to the captain by the cruise director. The captain whom I worked with before was a pretty good guy. Would he axe me, was the question.

It was funny because he wasn't really mad. He was just, I could tell, smiling underneath it all. He could imagine all that might have taken place and being Italian probably wished he was in my shoes. He told us both to go to our cabin.

It was a strange twist of irony at the time because that girl who came on the ship in Monte Carlo he had his eyes on. Her and I were pretty good friends by this time. We would have chats together or go ashore and see some sights together. There was no pressure with her unlike the others whom I felt the pressure from or was giving the pressure to. It was quite nice actually.

So the girl I wanted was going out with the previous captain and this captain was interested in a girl that was not too interested in him, with whom I hung around. So off to our cabins we went to await the outcome.

Dinner service was fast approaching and there was still no word. I worked dinner. I worked breakfast the next day. I worked the lunch and another dinner.

Not even one person reprimanded me. Meanwhile, the girl I had a hankering for I never saw again. She disembarked a few days later at the end of her contract but not without being blackmailed, I am afraid. It is funny how one can appear to remain faithful but in the end to do so you have to be unfaithful. How bizarre is that! Such was ship life.

Another strange incident occurred during the contract. About a month earlier when we had transitioned from Asia to the Mediterranean there was some talk of me becoming maître d'. I wasn't sure how I felt about the idea. It would be more money for sure, but whether I wanted the responsibility was another question. I knew I could do it, but maybe later, I thought. However, it looked more and more like I was going to be maître d', so I was ready to accept the offer. But as fate would have it, I was dealt a cruel blow before my promotion.

I got the only complaint I ever had while on the ship. In fact, outside of this complaint, I hardly remember anything that compared to this one.

For some stupid reason during this time we were short on waiters. The dining room was set up so there would be four stations, each of which consisted of one front waiter and one back waiter. The front waiter took care of the order taking and clearing and placing of the plates when they came out of the kitchen while the back waiter or runner as we like to call them used to take the order left for him on the station and pick up the food in the back. Teamwork was important. Communication was vital. That is why I was sent home so quickly on the previous contract because a man short in the dining room makes it very difficult for service.

So this particular cruise I was on my own during the evening service. The complaint began when I was putting the soup down in front of this lady. She suddenly moved her arm and knocked some soup on her dress. Horrified, she started to get real upset with me. No amount of apology on my behalf would suffice.

Throughout this torturous seven-day cruise, she avoided me like the plague and whenever she got a chance told everyone how horrible a waiter I really was to spill something on her dress. To my relief, other passengers knew she was going on way too long about this. So much so that they were coming up telling me not to worry and that I was a fine waiter. Sometimes when people say that it goes a long way.

Having spent a lot of money at a clothing store in Sorrento, I discovered that the job had gone to someone else. I wasn't too impressed by that and decided that I would never become a maître d' if they asked me again. The complaint had got back to head office. I received no help from the maître d' or hotel manager in this turn of events. I thought they should have at least mentioned all the rave reviews I was getting from everyone else.

You could say during this contract a lot of things were going on. A lot of personalities were involved, but that was ship life. The parties, boozing, and visiting all the sites as we went from one port to the next was unforgettable. It was fun, to say the least.

Another port I enjoyed was Ashdod. That day I had the chance to see Bethlehem and Jerusalem. A full day tour. That was amazing!

Just before my contract was about to end, we were in Sorrento, Italy again. Seems like a lot of things happened in Sorrento!

The girl who came on the ship in April, and was becoming a really good friend, asked me for my address so we could keep in touch. Usually it was always me that was asking for the addresses of girls and here was one asking for mine. That was quite the turnaround for me.

However with my poor record of choosing girls, to my credit, I told her that no way I was keeping in touch with anyone long distance anymore because I had decided that I was not returning to the ship. Looking back it was pretty mean of me to say such a thing, but I really had no intention of returning. She said okay and returned later and gave me a key chain she bought. I promised to leave her my pillow I brought with me on board for my stiff necks. I left it in my cabin so she could grab it.

I had enough of ship life and figured I had seen pretty much all I wanted to see. The traveling life was coming to an end for me. That was it. I literally had been on the go since 1979 when I took a bartending course. The travel, partying, living out of a suitcase was getting tiresome.

I disembarked on July 1st, 1995 in Civitavecchia, Italy expecting never to return and begin my life on land in Victoria B.C.

Okay, One More Time

When I left the ship on July 1, I had decided that I wasn't going to return to the ship. I was going to settle down once and for all in beautiful British Columbia. I'd find a good job in a nice dining room. I already had my bachelor apartment waiting for me that was being occupied by my mother. She was cashing in on the free rent I was paying while on the ship so she could save and move back east.

She actually left to go back east before I touched down in Vancouver, so I could have my place back. This place I lived in was so small that when my friend came to visit that summer he slept on the pull out couch. The next morning in order to get to the bathroom he had to get up and we had to put the couch back to its normal position in order to enter it. I slept on a Murphy bed out of the wall.

It was summer time and it dawned on me that two months holiday then returning to the ship sounded a lot better than actually looking for work. I mean, really when it came right down to it, I was hooked on the ship. Also, when I took a minute and looked at the jobs available, it was enough for me to phone Fort Lauderdale and ask them to schedule me on another contract. I chose the same ship I left because the plan was it would be heading to the Caribbean in the fall.

I was beginning to understand why some people never leave the ship to go back on dry land. Everything is taken care of for you. No bills, no car trouble, and I could save a bunch of money. I know it was six months without a day off but I was used to it and it was fun. I guess that is everything that ever mattered to me. If I cannot have fun where I work, I don't stick around very long.

As well, I felt that there might have been a good chance to eventually meet someone. I wanted to settle, but not with someone from Canada anymore. I didn't really share anything in common with the girls I would meet when I came home.

So with my plans in place to return to the ship, I strolled down to the travel agent to book a holiday. I chose England, Ireland, Wales, and Scotland. I had to pick up the stuff I left at the Bed and Breakfast in Penzance when I broke my wrist a couple of years earlier. The only communication with them since then was that postcard from Myrtle Beach the previous summer.

I hung around Victoria the first couple of weeks before heading out. I had this apartment for about a week before I headed out to Singapore, so I wanted to get to know the area.

My usual routine was waking up and heading down the street to have my breakfast at this diner. Then I'd head to the store and pick up some snacks to have during the day. Next I'd head down to the water just a block away and read while sunbathing. I read a couple of books. Then off to a pub or restaurant for dinner and out that evening. As much as I was a people-person on the ship, when I was on holiday I became a bit reclusive.

I walked everywhere. It had been almost ten years that I hadn't owned a car.

One time I rented one to go up island to do some whale watching. Went as far up as Tofino where I stayed at a B&B for a night. The Pacific Ocean is quite cold even in the summer this far North. The water averages about 10 Celsius year-round, but I was lucky enough to have a warm sunny day. Swimming in the Pacific that day was fun, to say the least.

I headed to the United Kingdom, starting off in Glasgow. Travelling around by train on my Brit Rail pass, I headed to the west coast sleeping in Bed and Breakfast places. I saw Isle of Skye, Oban, Maillag, to name a few places. The train rides were beautiful. Travelling through the Scottish Highlands there was always a bit of a misty rain falling with the cloud cover quite low. The grass was the greenest I have ever seen anywhere dotted with sheep grazing about.

Scotland is one of those places where there is no hustle bustle. Life just seemed like a slower pace than what I was accustomed. Wales was even slower. I stopped by in Cardiff.

Then I headed to Ireland. A few years back in Jasper, if you recall, I was in touch with this Irish girl. After I asked her to come for a visit and she refused I decided to pass up keeping in touch with her. She made it clear she was getting married soon to another guy.

Well, I thought perhaps I would look her up anyway. I knew where she had worked so I decided to give a call to the hotel where she was back a few years ago, just to see if she was still there. This girl picked up the phone. Now don't forget I never talked to anyone with whom she worked with before to that minute. I asked if she still worked there. The person at the other end of the line said that she had left a couple of years ago.

I said okay then asked if she ever got married. I explained that I was from Canada and knew her and that I was in town passing through. At that moment I detected a silence on the other end. She told me to wait a minute and that she would give me her number to contact her. I was somewhat taken aback. I didn't expect that.

I called this number and she answered. Surprised to hear from me, I visited her for the day. She showed me around her town and I left saying

How I Took a Bartending Course and Traveled for Seventeen Years

I would drop a line when I got back home. I did but she never answered, of course. But it was the hug I got when we said goodbye that was surprising. When I departed I felt good about seeing her again. She was happily married and for some reason I felt as happy moving on. Heading back to the ship, I was wondering what would be in store for me once I got back.

Just before flying out of London I went to the Bed and Breakfast and picked up my stuff. Telling the owners of my adventures the past couple of years they just started to shake their heads especially at all the places I had visited.

It was September 1995 and I was 36 years old. I was ready to head back to the ship for another contract. This was my life now and nothing was going to change it. I was in my prime, having overcome some injuries on a couple of contracts to my sciatic nerve and feet soreness. Here comes that Condo in Myrtle Beach, I thought.

The End of the Beginning

I headed to the Mediterranean to join the ship I left two months earlier. Joining up with most of the people I had left it was like fitting into an old shoe.

Work was going well. I was at the top of my game. The comment cards complimenting me were numerous and the team we had in the dining room was amazing. I was getting excited about the upcoming trans-Atlantic voyage once again.

But then a strange set of coincidences took place that I really had no control over. It was like so many things that happened to me before in previous years that just took me in a totally different direction. A direction I least expected.

It started only about a month in the contract when there was a big party in the crew mess for those disembarking. One of the people leaving happened to be the stewardess who wanted my address before I left the last time. I remember having a dance with her then awkwardly saying goodbye. I was feeling kind of bad about how I brushed her off that day in Sorrento.

Anyway, all that didn't matter. She was leaving and she had mentioned she probably wouldn't be returning either so I figured that was a lost cause. I wasn't going to ask now for her address. All I could think about was lying on the beach every Saturday in Barbados.

Then about 30 minutes before an evening service was about to begin the maître d' informed me the hotel manager wanted to see me. Wondering what this was all about, I headed up to his office where I found out they needed a maître d' on another ship and they were sending me there.

After their chance to have me during the last contract and telling me to go buy the suits then changing their mind, I refused the promotion this time around. We bickered back and forth. I said I was happy where I was and he said to me I was ready for maître d' and that I didn't have a choice in the matter. As he put it, when the student is ready, the teacher will appear.

I was scheduled to finish my shift that night and the next day disembark in Casablanca where I would stay overnight, then fly to Istanbul and stay another overnight then be picked up by the agent and head for Kusadasi, a Turkish resort.

How I Took a Bartending Course and Traveled for Seventeen Years

I started to warm up to the idea of becoming a maître d'. On a small ship like this one, with only 114 passengers, I would be responsible for the pool deck, bar, and dining room and any other food and beverage related functions. It wasn't that hard, but I had to make sure the guests were happy. I already knew my way around pretty well after a few contracts as a waiter.

I succeeded quite nicely. We received very high ratings and a lot of that was due to my hands-on approach in the dining room. Helping out the waiters was natural for me. I helped to get more bread and pour water or run some food. Whatever needed to be done I did, all the while chatting with the guests.

When evening service was coming to an end, the chef and I would head up to the bar and have a drink or two. Then we would be buying drinks for some of the guests as well. For example, those who were celebrating a birthday. The passengers loved us.

Each officer was given a $200 expense account for drinks each month. A lot of officers did not use any of their expense account as they never frequented the bar at all. So after the first week when the chef's and I accounts were full, the purser would put our drinks on an unused account. By the end of the month everyone's account was maxed out thanks to the chef and me. It was hilarious! Every night we would just head to the bar then afterwards there would be a pool party or another party going on in another cabin. It was party central!

Especially after we appeared in the crew show. I was Fred Astaire doing "Singing in the Rain." I also sang "My Way." Once the crew show was over midway through the cruise, you could say there was absolute approval for the dining room. The passengers ate it up and I was loving the adulation from the guests afterwards.

Soon after, the ship I was on was going to dry dock in Piraeus, Greece just outside of Athens for a couple of weeks. This usually meant there was going to be a change of crew before we headed out on the five-week crossing to Asia.

While on dry dock the buzz was always about who was coming aboard. The hairdresser noted that this stewardess from Iceland was joining the ship. "She seems like a nice girl, Steven," she said to me. It was that girl again that left the ship saying she wasn't coming back just like I did the previous time.

What had happened was when she returned to Iceland she had a change of mind and decided to do one more contract if she could go to Asia. It was that or not return. She got her request. The ship that was going to Asia was the one I got transferred to from Casablanca. How serendipitious!

Before she left Iceland she had heard I was on the ship. When she arrived she gave me a T-Shirt from Iceland. I thanked her. This was new for me. Someone actually getting me something and showing interest rather than me doing all the chasing; this was something new. "Okay," I thought, "now what do I do?"

I knew that if I was going to date this girl that would be it for me. All the girls before were nice but the timing and coincidental meetings with this girl were different. She was very nice and extremely popular.

Dry dock ended and we were on our way. The first time we got the chance we went to shore together in Limassol, Cyprus and shared some laughs over a Mad comic. Then we headed through the Suez Canal and onto Egypt. She was probably the first girl I met up to then who was more interested in me than herself. I guess that was the clincher right there. Someone actually put their thoughts of me before their own. Maybe that is how you can tell if you found the right one. Anyway I was quite liking it!

The big make or break moment came in Sharm el Sheik. It was a couple of nights before that the chef mentioned to me that this girl from Iceland seemed pretty interested in me. I thought that, yes, it appeared she was, but I was too cool and wanted to keep my options open. I didn't want to commit myself to anyone too early in the voyage. As maître d' I had my own cabin now. The good times and the women would be coming in throngs now that I had my own cabin.

During our day in Sharm el Sheik, I was out with the boys doing the walk into town. The girl from Iceland was tagging along when the bunch of waiters suddenly hailed a taxi for a ride the rest of the way. She then asked me if I would rather walk with her or join the others in the taxi. I hesitated for a moment that might have felt like five minutes. If I was younger I would have hopped in that taxi no problem. It meant more to be with the guys back then, but now not so much.

That is when I said, "you guys go ahead, I will walk." Because I chose to walk the course of my life changed.

Afterwards, she told me that if I had jumped in the taxi that was the end of the road for me. The next day my closet door was hanging from its hinge and she commented that I should get it fixed. I said, "Sure I will just tell the chief officer and he will send someone to fix it." After lunch that day I came back to the cabin and it was fixed. I wondered who fixed it. She was there and said she had fixed it. "Wow," I thought, "someone who is handier than I as well. She is really smart!"

That night she moved into the cabin. I couldn't be without her. I spent all my time with her and when I worked I could hardly wait to be with her.

While on the ship she bought a ticket for Canada and turned down a chance at a better position with the cruise line as a shore excursion manager. It would have meant a transfer to another ship for sure and an end to our relationship. We had our first date off the ship on New Year's Eve in Phuket Thailand. When we had an overnight in Jakarta we actually stayed in a hotel for the night hurrying back to the ship to make 7AM breakfast. Although I only had 4 months left when she returned to the ship we talked a lot about different things. She was the one for sure.

My contract expired on March 10, 1996 in Singapore. She still had a couple of months left before she left in June. While on the ship I faxed her a marriage proposal. She said yes and we were married on August 24th, 1996 over 17 years ago.

We wanted to go back together on the ship but were told it would be different ships so we started to make our life on land together rather than be separated at sea.

Life is amazing sometimes. Up to that time I did a lot of things most people just dream about doing but there comes a time when you have got to plant yourself. It was quite a while coming for me, but when it did, I knew she was the one for me.

Good thing she decided a couple of years earlier when she took a photo of the ship in St. Thomas that she wanted to work on one and good thing the hotel manager insisted I go to the other ship as maître d.

They say opposites attract but that may not be entirely true. I think two different people willing to accept each other's strengths and weaknesses attract each other. That was what happened to my wife and I. I was by then too set in my ways to change and she was as well. But thankfully we both were not selfish people.

All I can say is I went through many to figure it out. The jobs, the moves, travelling on a budget, and heartbreaks here and there. It ended up alright!

Today we are still happily married and have two great kids. I live a very normal life compared to those crazy days back when I was laying my head in a donut shop hung over back in 1982. I still wait on tables as does my wife. We have moved around a bit during the past 18 years but not nearly so much as you may think.

At 55 years of age, I am quite content watching and spending time with the family.

Epilogue

A lot of events happened because of that Bartending Course I took back in 1979.

Many decisions I made turned out to be pretty dumb when I look back, but at the time they all seemed pretty good. If I didn't go ahead with my ideas then I would have lived life not knowing the outcome. What is worse? A decision that went wrong or living life not knowing? I always liked the risk rather than living with the regret of not finding out.

I learned one thing throughout it all. When something turned wrong it was always because something better was waiting for me.

There are many people I met during these years to whom I owe a great thanks. It always seemed that I would meet someone or find a job just in the nick of time. I was always lucky in that respect and still am.

Looking back, it was a different time than it is now. I feel fortunate to have done the things I did when it wasn't so hard to do them. Times were a lot simpler then than they are now it seems, but maybe I am just getting older.

Of course, it may not surprise you that when I got married I had more jobs the first five years than all this book combined. However, that is another story. We moved from Victoria to Vancouver in British Columbia, then London to Guelph Ontario where we are now.

It was tough to adjust after traveling around and working on the cruise ship. I thought once we got settled, life would just continue along with both of us having fun and traveling. I started a few businesses that didn't turn out so well. After experiencing work as a Maitre'd I thought the job opportunities would be plentiful but they were not in the Hospitality Industry.

It was a difficult time accepting the fact that I may have seemed great elsewhere but I was a nobody in my own country.

But through it all my wife and I have stayed strong and our kids are having fun. Our hope is that we can teach them to move forward and seek out their dreams like I did when I took that bartending course way back in 1979!